Applied Humanism

Applied Humanism

How to Create More Effective and Ethical Businesses

Jennifer Hancock

BEP BUSINESS EXPERT PRESS

Applied Humanism: How to Create More Effective and Ethical Businesses

Copyright © Business Expert Press, LLC, 2019.

First published in 2019 by
Business Expert Press, LLC
222 East 46th Street, New York, NY 10017
www.businessexpertpress.com

ISBN-13: 978-1-94999-142-0 (paperback)
ISBN-13: 978-1-94999-143-7 (e-book)

Business Expert Press Business Ethics and Corporate Citizenship Collection

Collection ISSN: 2333-8806 (print)
Collection ISSN: 2333-8814 (electronic)

Cover and interior design by Exeter Premedia Services Private Ltd., Chennai, India

First edition: 2019

10 9 8 7 6 5 4 3 2 1

Printed in the United States of America.

Abstract

There is a reason why many business schools around the world are starting to teach humanistic management. Humanism, as a philosophy, helps us prioritize human value as important. This, in turn, supports good decision making and the positive interpersonal relationships that are the foundation of good collaborative and respectful decision making. Since all businesses are in the business of solving problems, good problem solving is essential to good business.

I don't think you can understand humanistic business management unless you understand what Humanism is. This book provides a short introduction to the philosophy of Humanism and discusses how and why it is being applied to business and why it is so effective when you do so. This book will help answer the questions: "What exactly is Humanism and why is it suddenly so popular? More importantly, how can we apply it to our businesses and other endeavors."

Humanism has already transformed many other disciplines including psychology, medicine, nursing, and more. Additionally, Humanism is foundational to the practice of human resources, without which businesses cannot operate. It is important for business managers to understand the philosophy fully so they can understand how to not only manage people more effectively, but how to operate their businesses in a way that helps the communities in which they operate. This book will provide the primer they need to create more effective and ethical businesses.

Keywords

humanism; humanist; humanistic; business; business management; decision making; critical thinking

Abstract

Contents

Introduction

Why This Book

This book is about humanistic business management. Specifically, it is about the Humanist philosophy and how it applies to the business of business.

Humanism is a philosophic approach to living life and solving problems. It is about taking responsibility for solving the problems we have and doing so in a way that is respectful of other people and of the environment because we are dependent on our environment for life. This sounds wonderful, but it requires critical thinking and personal responsibility to implement. The upside is that it has some very tangible positive impacts on how we go about the business of business.

We need Humanism in business because we live in a diverse global society. The biggest businesses are global, our commerce is global, thanks to the Internet, our friendships are increasing global. Our food, thankfully, is global as well (I am a big fan of Peruvian, Indian, and Columbian food, for instance).

All this global diversity has benefits, but like all good things, it has a downside as well. How we chose to manage the benefits versus the drawbacks will dictate our success going into the future.

People who are afraid of all this globalization see the downside, and it scares them. People who are for globalization are looking at the upside and think it outweighs the downside. Blind fear does not lead to good decisions, but neither does blind optimism.

Humanism, because it is focused on our common human morality, can help us cut across religious and cultural differences to find a common moral language and framework to help us work together despite our differences. It encourages us to recognize the humanity of those we disagree with so that we can recognize and explore their moral reasoning to find areas of common ground.

Humanism is also reality based. We do not like to make decisions based on assumptions, we want good science-based information. Without that, we are adrift.

The goal of Humanism is well-being or human flourishing. What is the point of life if we do not live it fully.

Finally, a humanistic mindset helps us recognize that we are all dependent on the society in which we live. Our businesses rely on customers, and those customers live somewhere and need food, water, shelter, health care, and a sense of community to thrive so that they can be our customers. Everywhere in the world this is true.

Humanism in business matters because humans matter. Businesses and commerce define how we interact with each other. We can either use our businesses to help humanity progress to more peaceful flourishing communities or we can allow our societies to be consumed with greed. We can balance profit and benefit to society. And, we must. This is why, Humanism matters.

About the Author

My name is Jennifer Hancock, I am your author and guide. I was raised in a Humanist household and have spent my adult life working for Humanist groups and educating people about the philosophy. I am considered one of the most prominent writers and speakers in the world of Humanism today.

Using Science and Philosophy to Create Happier Workplaces

One of the main goals of Humanism is to create human flourishing. Happiness is of specific concern to us. Because happiness matters, happy workplaces matter.

The Humanist prescription for happiness is so universal and so simple that even a child can articulate it. When I was 11, I wrote the following motto for myself: live life fully, love other people, and leave the world a better place. Every major religion and philosopher throughout history has taught basically the same thing because this prescription works.

Happiness or well-being is a difficult metric to measure because it means different things to different people. I take a utilitarian approach. To me, happiness occurs when my stress levels are low and I feel "in control."

In the workplace, this means I feel happy when I feel respected, when the work that I do matters, and when problem-solving is fun, not frustrating, meaning we solve problems collaboratively and in the best interest of the company and our customers.

Respect, mattering, and problem-solving are intertwined and combined. They align with our prescription for happiness, well-being, loving other people, and leaving the world a better place. And, all rely on a combination of philosophy and science to implement.

This prescription for workplace happiness is not simply a feel-good method. Humanism, as a methodology, can be tested for outcomes. Humanists choose this approach because it yields what most people consider to be good results. Taking a humanistic approach to business directly impacts the quality of the work being done and constitutes a moral and pragmatic imperative for the workplace.

The Benefits of Taking a Humanistic Approach

I realize a lot of people are in business just to make money, and well-being and happiness is an afterthought. But, last I checked, no one is going to give you money just because you asked for it. Most people will only give you money if you solve their problems well.

All businesses are in the business of solving problems. If you are not solving problems, you are not in business. The businesses that do the best help their customers solve a problem in a way that works and is cost effective.

Our business objective should be the making of good decisions so that we problem-solve well. To that end, we need a philosophic tweak to how we think about our businesses and our jobs. The goal? Making the world a better place by helping people solve their problems so that we can create societies where people, all people, flourish.

A work group can't solve problems well unless they respect each other and have a shared set of values that helps them collaboratively judge what a good solution is. It helps if they all understand why getting the solution right matters so they are motivated to find good solutions to your customer's problems.

The purpose of creating happier more humanistic workplace cultures is so problem-solving is truly collaborative and everyone's input is respected.

To find good solutions to our problems, we must create workplaces where everyone is treated with dignity and worth, and the group is cohesive and not divisive.

The reason it is hard to create cohesive work groups is because we humans are instinctually tribal and divisive. To overcome this, we need to take practical pro-active steps to overcome our tribal brain. The best way to do that is to encourage people to think more humanistically and less tribally.

As a Humanist, I approach all problem-solving as both an ethical exercise and a pragmatic one. Ethics help me determine what a good solution looks like. Science helps ensure that whatever solution I find will actually work. We need both science and ethical philosophy to create better, more cohesive work groups that problem-solve well.

Here is why. Ethical philosophy encourages us to treat each other with dignity. Science validates the need for dignity and respect in group problem-solving. Behavioral science in particular can help us create workplace cultures where dignity and respect are the norm. It turns out one of the necessary conditions to do that, according to science, is through philosophic training that reinforces dignity as a primary value.

There is a reason why many business schools around the world are starting to teach humanistic management. Humanism, as a philosophy, helps us prioritize human dignity and worth as important. This approach is validated by science, which almost always reinforces taking a humanistic approach to problem-solving. In fact, we often cannot implement a solution that works unless we take a humanistic approach.

For example: let us consider the problem of bullying and harassment in the workplace. We need to tackle the problem of bullying, because if we do not, we will not have respectful workplaces, and that has negative cascading effects on not only the general levels of happiness and well-being in the workplace, but the work itself and problem-solving specifically.

Our ideal is respectful collaborative problem-solving. Realistically, businesses usually solve problems based on who is the loudest, who is the biggest bully, people's insecurities, and more. It is time we recognize that bullying management is bad management and stop rewarding it.

Stopping harassment and bullying is both a moral and a practical good. To solve this problem, we need science because we need practical solutions. The good news is we have seven plus decades of scientific research on how to stop unwanted behavior, like bullying.

If we pay attention to the science, we know what we need to do to get bullying to stop. Stop rewarding it and start rewarding the behavior we do want. To do that effectively, we need to be more compassionate.

People do not do this because it seems counterintuitive, but it is true. Treating a bully with dignity and compassion allows us to behaviorally train them to stop. In fact, it is probably impossible to stop bullying if you do not approach it humanistically. Seven decades of behavioral science validates this.

This brings us full circle. Humanistic philosophy makes us want to stop bullying, science tells us how to get it to stop. Applying a humanistic mindset helps us to actually do it.

Humanistic philosophy and science allow us to do what is right and what will work in a way that is professional, compassionate, ethical, and effective.

We need to be more strategic in our problem-solving and really take the time to view the research on what works and what does not. This applies to everything! All aspects of life.

Creating workplaces where people are treated with dignity, the work matters and the problem-solving is done well requires us to combine both ethical humanistic philosophy with applied science to get solutions that actually work.

This approach helps us to live life fully, love other people, and leave the world a better place in our business and personal life. Imagine the positive impact we can have if we succeed in creating truly happy workplaces that make a positive difference for our customers and our communities.

What Is in This Book?

This book is broken into four sections.

Section 1: What Is Humanism?

It is difficult to understand the hows and whys of humanistic business management without understanding the philosophy at the core of the practice.

Section 2: Applying Humanism to the World of Business
There are several aspects of the Humanist philosophy that are relevant to business management, and in this section, we will be discussing how to apply the different aspects of the philosophy to our business practices.

Section 3: Problem-Solving Like a Humanist
This section is an overview of critical thinking techniques and how Humanists combine critical thinking with moral reasoning to generate ethical and effective results.

Section 4: Case Studies
This section provides examples of how a Humanist approaches problem-solving in a business context using chronic business and human resources problems as examples.

PART I

What Is Humanism?

CHAPTER 1

Introduction

This part of the book will provide you with a quick overview of the philosophy of Humanism.

Humanism is one of the most influential and yet, most misunderstood philosophies of all time. Unfortunately, most people do not know anything about it. To make matters worse, there are a lot of misconceptions about what this philosophy is exactly. This chapter is designed to introduce the philosophy and explain its major tenets.

No Proselytizing

Disclaimer: Humanism is a philosophy. Some of you may agree with this philosophy. Some of you may not. That is OK. The purpose of this chapter is to introduce the philosophy, not to convert you to it.

Many people are Humanists or humanistically inclined. If you read this and find yourself agreeing with it. Great. I hope this book will help you clarify your personal philosophy.

If you read this book and find it annoys or upsets you because you do not agree with anything in it, that is fine too. Not everyone is a Humanist. I am not out to change your mind. There is no dogma to Humanism. This philosophy either makes sense to you or it does not. If it turns out this does not make sense to you, what I hope you take away from this book is a basic level of knowledge about what the Humanist philosophy is so that you can better understand why people are talking about and promoting a humanistic approach to business.

Some people who read this book will agree with only some parts and disagree with other parts. Again, that is fine too. Humanism is a philosophy. You are free to take from it what you want and ignore the stuff that you do not like. All I can do is explain the philosophy as it is currently understood by practicing Humanists. It is not a requirement that you agree with everything in this book. In fact—thinking explicitly about why you do not agree with me—is a useful exercise.

Many people reading this will agree with Humanist morality, but disagree with our rejection of the supernatural. If this describes you, you can consider yourself humanistically inclined if that makes you happy, and there is a long tradition of this sort of hybrid approach. It is perfectly fine.

A Word About Nomenclature

The term Humanist (with a capital H) was coined in the early 1900s to describe a specifically non-theistic approach to morality. People who apply this philosophy and morality to their theistic or religious beliefs use the term humanistic as an adjective to describe their approach to belief (e.g., Humanistic Judaism, Humanistic Christianity, Humanistic Buddhism, and so forth).

Humanism is the philosophy. Humanists are people who practice the philosophy. humanistic is the application of the philosophy to various human endeavors (e.g., humanistic medicine, humanistic business management, humanistic nursing, humanistic psychology, humanistic religion, and so forth)

The word Humanist refers to a strictly secular approach. Humanistic may include a more hybrid approach.

What You Need to Know

This section is designed to be a short and hopefully sweet introduction to the philosophy of Humanism, hitting on all the important bits, including:

- What Humanism is
- What Humanists care about
- How we go about solving our problems
- Why we believe our way of thinking about the world is better than the alternatives
- Why, if you are a Humanist, you should probably admit it to yourself and to others

Because Humanism arises in every culture, and in every time, there is, quite literally, more information than you could ever possibly read to help you explore the philosophy further. If, after reading this book, you want to learn more, there are international, national, and local organizations of Humanists that you can reach out to and get to know. In addition, there are many online groups you can participate in. You can also choose to do nothing with the information you read in this book.

CHAPTER 2

What Is Humanism and Why Should I Care?

To put it simply, Humanism is one of the most powerful forces for positive social change on the planet. Some of the most famous and influential people in our society have been and continue to be Humanists. The Humanist philosophy provided the foundation for most of the social and civil justice movements of the past century, as well as providing the philosophical foundation for democracy and science.

Quite literally, if it were not for Humanists, Europe would still be in the Dark Ages. America would probably have not been *discovered* by Europeans, and everyone everywhere would still be trying to cook with fire. And no, I am not exaggerating.

The modern world has been shaped and made possible by the dominance of humanistic ideas. This is exactly why it is so stunning that most people have no idea what it is.

What Is Humanism?

One of the main reasons Humanism is so poorly understood is that it has no standard definition. Yet, it is instantly recognizable once you grasp its central ideas. It is a very simple philosophy that has some very profound implications for how you view your place in the universe. As one of my friends in Saudi Arabia once pointed out, it is not rocket science. If you spend just a little bit of time thinking about what morality and ethics mean to us as humans without the prescriptions of religion and divine revelation, Humanism is probably what you are going to come up with.

Regardless, this is a book about Humanism, so perhaps, I should provide you with something more concrete to wrap your mind around.

Defining Humanism

The American Humanist Association currently defines Humanism as "a progressive philosophy of life, that without supernaturalism, affirms our ability and responsibility to lead ethical lives of personal fulfillment that aspire to the greater good of Humanity."

In other words, it is a way of thinking about ethics that emphasizes both our personal development and our moral obligations. We have a moral responsibility to try to thrive as individuals and to create societies in which all people can flourish. Or, as I like to say: live life fully, love other people, and leave the world a better place.

Putting It Another Way

According to the International Humanist and Ethical Union's (IHEU) Amsterdam Declaration of 2002,

> *Humanism is the outcome of a long tradition of free thought that has inspired many of the world's great thinkers and creative artists and gave rise to science itself.*

According to the IHEU, there are seven fundamental elements of Humanism:

- *Humanism is ethical:* Humanists have a duty to care for all of humanity, including future generations.
- *Humanism is rational:* Humanism advocates the application of the methods of science and free inquiry to the problems of human welfare.
- *Humanism supports democracy and human rights:* The principles of democracy and human rights can be applied to many human relationships and are not restricted to the methods of government.
- *Humanism insists that personal liberty must be combined with social responsibility:* Humanism ventures to build a world on the idea of the free person responsible to society.

- *Humanism is a response to the widespread demand for an alternative to dogmatic religion*: Humanism recognizes that reliable knowledge of the world and ourselves arises through a continuing process of observation, evaluation, and revision.
- *Humanism values artistic creativity and imagination*: Humanism affirms the importance of literature, music, and the visual and performing arts for personal development and fulfillment.
- *Humanism is a life stance aimed at maximizing our personal fulfillment through the cultivation of ethical and creative living*: It offers an ethical and rational means of addressing the challenges of our time.

What Do Humanists Want?

The goal of a Humanist has remained the same since Aristotle. Eudaimonia, a Greek word commonly translated as happiness or welfare; however, *human flourishing* has been proposed as a more accurate translation. Eudaimonia consists of two words: it consists of the words "eu" ("good") and "daimōn" ("spirit").

Aristotle described Eudaimonia as the highest human good. It was and is the aim of both practical and political philosophies. Meaning, it was about both what the individual should aspire to and what we should be aiming for as a society.

As a Humanist named Steven Schafersman once wrote:

> *Humanists stand for the building of a more humane, just, compassionate, and democratic society using a pragmatic ethics based on human reason, experience, and reliable knowledge-an ethics that judges the consequences of human actions by the well-being of all life on Earth.*
> *—Steven Schafersman,*
> *Geologist, Humanist and Science Advocate.*

Keep It Simple Stupid

By now your head is probably spinning. One of the problems we Humanists have in explaining our philosophy is that it is deceptively simple, yet wonderfully complex. There is no easy way to describe it.

Regardless, I will give you a synopsis in plain English, understanding that we will be going into more detail on these basic elements in the following chapters.

Humanism is a philosophy that is primarily focused on how we as individuals can be good human beings. We seek to be ethical, moral, and compassionate people in all that we do. However, we also understand that good moral reasoning requires us to think clearly and rationally about the problems we face, so Humanists are as much concerned with how we think, as we are concerned with what we think about. To that end, we practice the related skills of free thought, critical thinking, and logic.

Humanists are firmly convinced that we are in control of our own destinies, and that we can choose to act in a way that will improve our lives and the lives of others. We refuse to be victims of fate. For this reason, Humanism is a philosophy that focuses on the future. We are not content with the status quo, as we are always pushing ourselves to make things better.

How we define "better" is critical to understanding the philosophy of Humanism. Humanists judge the outcomes using compassion-based morality, and we are totally unapologetic about that. If it helps humans, it is a good outcome. If it hurts, it is bad. Absent from our thinking and reasoning is anything that could be considered supernatural or religious.

We do not consider religious or supernatural ideas to be a sound basis for moral reasoning. Our concern for the welfare of others is sufficient, and we have no need for any external or supernatural sanction for our moral values. We are, in fact, convinced that religious reasoning, however well-intentioned it may be, tends to cause more harm than good because it encourages dogmatic adherence to a set of rules, instead of acknowledging the necessity of judging each situation on its own merits.

In other words, without supernaturalism, Humanists seek to lead ethical lives of personal fulfillment that aspire to the greater good of humanity. We do this by applying reason and logic to our feelings of compassion with a determination to actively work to make things better not just for ourselves, but for everyone.

CHAPTER 3

A Short History of Humanism

Now that you know a little bit about the philosophy, the next question is: how long has Humanism been around? The answer is that Humanism has probably been around as long as there have been humans. And, as long as Humanism has been around, there have been people who demonize it. This is interesting because, really, it is not like Humanism is some radical idea. Well, actually, it is. More on that later.

My point is that people keep re-inventing Humanism for themselves. All it takes is for a compassionate person to spend some time thinking about morality, the universe, and everything without religion and he or she will usually come up with something that is either Humanism or closely related to it. This process is happening all the time and has probably been happening throughout human history.

We do not really have historical records going back to the dawn of humanity. What we know about humanistic philosophies is limited to the historical era, otherwise known as the last 7,000 to 10,000 years.

Here is what we know. In every culture that is studied, including those that rely on an oral tradition (as opposed to written), we see evidence of humanistic thought. We see it in the writings of the ancient Sumerians and of the ancient Egyptians and in the oral traditions of American Indians and Arctic nomads.

However, when we get to about 600 BCE (Before the Common Era), we start to see specifically Humanist writings begin to appear all over the world. This development is probably more a function of us actually having these writings to refer to, rather than the lack of such thinkers earlier.

For a really great resource, check out www.humanistictexts.org that provides a wonderful collection of humanistic writings from various time periods and from all parts of the globe.

Let us review some of the main forms of Humanism that have developed over time.

Ancient Humanism

In India

There are two major philosophies that came out of ancient India that are either Humanist or humanistic in nature. They are Carvaka and Buddhism.

Let us start with Carvaka. This philosophy arose in India around 600 BCE and is both a skeptical and rationalistic philosophy. It rejected the supernatural and the Vedas and emphasized that this was the only life we have, so make the best of it.

> *While life is yours live joyously;*
> *No one can avoid Death's searching eye:*
> *When this body of ours is burnt,*
> *How can it ever return again?*

Buddhism is often considered a humanistic or Humanist philosophy depending on the form practiced. Many modern Humanists practice Buddhist meditation as a way to train and calm their minds. The aspects of Buddhism that are most like Humanism are its emphasis on finding balance and on compassion.

Happiness comes when your work and words are of benefit to yourself and others.

There are only two mistakes one can make along the road to truth: not going all the way, and not starting.

In China

In ancient China, there were at least two great Humanist teachers whose knowledge survives to this day. As in India, one is more famous than the other. These two philosophy teachers were Confucius and Mo Tzu.

Confucius (if he existed) lived around 500 BCE and was said to be a civil servant turned philosopher or teacher. His philosophy was as much concerned with cultivating virtue in individuals as it was with creating a virtuous government and society.

From the Great Learning

Acting according to our humanity provides the true path through life. Wisdom from the past helps us learn how to follow this path.

From the Analects

Tsze-lu asked what constituted the superior man. Confucius answered,

> *"The cultivation of himself in reverential carefulness."*
> *"And is this all?"*
> *"He cultivates himself so as to give rest to others."*
> *"And is this all?"*
> *"He cultivates himself so as to give rest to all the people."*

Mo Tzu was also a civil servant turned philosopher or teacher. He lived around 400 BCE and taught universal love and meritocracy, rather than aristocracy.

> *Mo Tzu said: The purpose of the Humanist is to be found in procuring benefits for the world and eliminating its calamities.*

> *Now, how is a doctrine to be examined?*

> *Mo Tzu said: Some standard of judgment must be established. To expound a doctrine without regard to the standard is similar to determining the directions of sunrise and sunset on a revolving potter's wheel. By such a means, the distinction of right and wrong, benefit and harm, cannot be known. Therefore there must be three tests.*

> *What are the three tests?*

> *Mo Tzu said: Its basis, its verifiability, and its applicability.*

The Greeks

The ancient Greeks had a lot of Humanists and humanistically inclined philosophers. For the sake of brevity, I am going to focus on just three: Socrates, Democritus, and Epicurus.

The most famous of these three is Socrates. As he is considered to be the founder of Western philosophy and of Western humanistic thought, we will start with him. He lived around 400 BCE and is most famous for his ethics and methods of discourse.

> Some one will say: And are you not ashamed, Socrates, of a course of life which is likely to bring you to an untimely end? To him I may fairly answer: There you are mistaken: a man who is good for anything ought not to calculate the chance of living or dying; he ought only to consider whether in doing anything he is doing right or wrong—acting the part of a good man or of a bad.

Democritus is pre-Socratic, meaning he lived before Socrates. He is considered to be the father of modern science because of his work on atoms. He was also an ardent defender of democracy as a form of government. Regardless, some of the most humanistic quotes from ancient Greece come from Democritus, so I am including several here just because I love what he had to say so much.

> Men find happiness neither by means of the body nor through possessions, but through uprightness and wisdom.

> It is hard to fight desire; but to control it is the sign of a reasonable man. Violent desire for one thing blinds the soul to all others. Immoderate desire is the mark of a child, not a man. If your desires are not great, a little will seem much to you; for small appetite makes poverty equivalent to wealth.

> Virtue does not consist of avoiding wrongdoing, but in having no wish to do wrong. It is a great thing, when one is in adversity, to think of duty. Refrain from crimes not through fear but through duty.

Believe not everything, but only what is proven: the former is foolish, the latter the act of a sensible man. Fools are shaped by the gifts of chance, but those who understand these things, by the gifts of wisdom.

Epicurus lived around 300 BCE and believed a man's purpose was to live a happy and peaceful life. He believed that good and evil are best judged by whether they bring pleasure or pain. His name is, to this day, synonymous with the pursuit of pleasure in the Western world. Humanists do not view him as a hedonist. We view him as an articulate proponent of the philosophy we share.

Death does not concern us, because as long as we exist, death is not here. And when it does come, we no longer exist.

It is folly for a man to pray to the gods for that which he has the power to obtain by himself.

Fast-Forward

Rather than continue on with a litany of humanistic thinkers and writers, I am going to give you my fast-forward version of Humanist history. What follows is a quick overview of the high points as I see them.

The Golden Age of Islam

Let us fast-forward to medieval Europe. It is in the Dark Ages. Christianity is dominant. It is basically a land lit only by fire. But in Arabia, Africa, and Asia, they are experiencing a golden age. This period, known as the Golden Age of Islam, lasted from about 700 CE to the 16th century. This was a period when scholars were studying all the ancient traditions from China, Persia, Greece, and India. And yes, they included the various humanist and humanistic traditions as part of their study. Because of the relative freedom of the sciences, Islamic culture flourished during this time.

Many people are surprised to find that there are indeed Humanist and humanistic traditions within the greater community of Islam. The fact is that there were full-on secular Humanists of great renown living during this period. For instance, Abu Bakr Al-Razi, a famous medical writer of the 9th century, believed that reason alone could give us certain knowledge, that all claims of revelation were false, and that religions were dangerous.

What is important to our understanding of the history of Humanism is that the scholars of Islam during its Golden Age were excited by, and were willing to learn from, other cultures.

> *We should not be ashamed to acknowledge truth from whatever source it comes to us, even if it is brought to us by former generations and foreign peoples. For him who seeks the truth there is nothing of higher value than truth itself.*
>
> —*Al-Kindi (c. 801-66)*

Islamic scholars spent a lot of time copying, translating, and studying the works of the *ancients*. And because they did that, those texts were available for Europeans to *rediscover* when they finally decided that they had had enough of living in ignorance, which brings us to the European Renaissance.

The Renaissance

If you did not learn about the European Renaissance in school or cannot remember much about it, except that it was in Europe and marked the end of the Dark Ages, here is how a Humanist views that period.

The Renaissance was a cultural movement that spanned a few hundred years. The hallmark of this period in Europe was that people started to take an interest in learning things again. Specifically, they were interested in learning the *classics*, which to them meant the ancient Greeks. Once people start learning, they tend to become voracious learners. As a result, over the course of a few centuries, Europe went from being a backwater place to being the center of learning and culture in the world. This did not make the Muslims very happy, but that is another story.

It was during the Renaissance when the term *humanist* started to be used. A Renaissance humanist was basically a scholar of the humanities. In hindsight, it was inevitable that the Renaissance Humanists, as they started to learn more and more about what other people thought and about the history of Christianity itself, would start to question the official dogma of the Catholic Church. As you might expect, the Catholic Church hierarchy was not exactly happy about this development. This brings us to the Reformation.

The Reformation

As learning became more widespread, the problem of controlling what people thought about religion got bigger and bigger. This struggle eventually resulted in the Reformation.

There were a wide variety of reasons why European reformers wanted to reform the Catholic Church. Some reasons were political; some were intellectual; some were theological. There was also the fact that the Catholic Church, at this time, was pretty corrupt. Regardless, people started to break away from the authority of the Catholic Church, and humanism was often invoked as a way to declare intellectual independence from the Catholic Church. There were wars, people died, and at the end of this period, people in Europe were basically free to believe whatever they wanted—more or less.

Enlightenment

Once people in Europe had freed their minds from religious control, scientists were able to pursue scientific truth where it led, and not just where the religious authorities thought it should go. I like to think of the Enlightenment as a period when, having won the basic right of freedom of belief, European intellectuals were now free to focus their attention on expanding scientific knowledge and on pursuing social issues that concerned them.

The Enlightenment was a mid-18th-century movement, and the hallmark of it was the idea that human reason was the only way to discern truth. Critical thinking, the challenging of arbitrary authority, and a strong belief in the power of rationality were hallmarks of the period. According to Immanuel Kant, the Enlightenment represented "Mankind's final coming of age, the emancipation of the human consciousness from an immature state of ignorance and error."

This period, which was basically a humanistic revolution, culminated in the American Revolution. As I wrote earlier, Humanist ideas are simple and straightforward, but that is precisely what makes them so revolutionary and radical.

Modern Age

Many historians think the Modern Age of humanism began with the publication of Thomas Paine's Age of Reason in the years 1794 to 1807 (when the final draft was done). This book was a product of the Enlightenment. It openly rejected the supernaturalism of the Bible. But more importantly, it directly attacked the authority of the Bible itself, treating the book as one would any other piece of literature. It was scandalous, but it was also a bestseller.

After that, more and more people started to write about the need for a morality based on something other than supernatural beliefs, and by 1853, the British Humanistic Religious Society was founded.

In 1877, the word *humanist* was used to describe Felix Adler, the founder of the Ethical Culture Society, which was formed to promote what is now known as Ethical Humanism.

In the 1920s, some Unitarian ministers started preaching a pragmatic nonreligious philosophy they called *Humanism*, and in 1929, Rev. Charles Francis Potter founded the First Humanist Society of New York. This organization still exists. Prominent members of its advisory board have included Albert Einstein, Julian Huxley, Helen Keller, and John Dewey.

In 1933, the first Humanist Manifesto was written and signed, and in 1941, the American Humanist Association was founded. In 1952, the International Humanist and Ethical Union was founded. That pretty much brings us up to the present, historically speaking.

What Has Humanism Done for You Lately?

If you like freedom of belief, then you can thank humanists like Erasmus, whose work during the Renaissance laid the philosophic foundation for the Reformation. If you like democracy, you can thank humanists such as John Locke, a key figure of the Enlightenment. If you like equal rights for all, then you can thank Humanists like A. Phillip Randolph and Helen Keller, who were instrumental in securing equal rights for minorities, women, and the disabled. (Note the capital Humanist for some and not others is intentional. Capital H Humanists—self-identified as Humanists and were/are active members of Humanist societies).

If you like having vaccines, antibiotics, and modern medicine, you should absolutely thank a Humanist. The list of Humanists who have made significant contributions to science and medicine is rather long and includes Crick and Watson (DNA) and Jonas Salk (polio vaccine). In fact, 22 currently living Nobel Laureates in science consider themselves to be Humanists.

As I said at the beginning of this book, modern life, as we know it, would not have been possible without Humanists. Basically, if it were not for Humanists, we would probably all still be living in the Dark Ages.

Well, actually, that is assuming your ancestors were living in Europe, because the rest of the world was not experiencing a Dark Age at all. However, if there were not any Humanists anywhere, Islam probably would not have had its Golden Age. If it had not been for Humanists exerting their influence somewhere, it is pretty safe to assume that everywhere would have been in a Dark Age, except we would not know about it because, well, we would not know any different.

Regardless, the point is that, if we are considering the impact Humanism has had on the history of Western culture and by extension the rest of the world, the European Renaissance, fueled by the philosophy of Humanism, had a tremendous impact on the world. We might not agree on whether that impact was positive or negative, given all the expansion, exploration, and exploitation that went on, but it certainly caused dramatic changes to occur just about everywhere. The quality of the science from the period of the Enlightenment, again, driven by Humanists in Europe and their counterparts around the world, gave us things like electricity and modern medicine. It is because of humanists that we are not all still trying to toast our bread over an open fire. Point made.

CHAPTER 4

Gratuitous Name Dropping

A lot of really famous and influential people are Humanists. In fact, if you remember a philosopher from ancient history, that is probably because they were either a Humanist or they were teaching a humanistic philosophy. The great thinkers and doers throughout history are often considered *great* precisely because they took a humanistic approach. We do not just claim Socrates, Buddha, and Confucius. We also had Marcus Aurelius (Roman Emperor and Stoic), Thomas Jefferson (President and Deist), and Voltaire (philosophical satirist and human rights activist).

However, there is one eensy-weensy-teeny little problem. Prior to the mid-1800s, no one called themselves a Humanist even if they were and the philosophy was not even described as a philosophy until the early 1900s. While we know from their writings that these *greats* were humanists or humanistically inclined, they did not actually call themselves Humanists or label their philosophy Humanism. As it is intellectually dishonest to ascribe a philosophy to people without their expressed consent, we cannot actually claim authoritatively that any of them were Humanists. The best we can do is say they appear to be humanists, or that they were promoting a humanistic philosophy in hindsight.

However, since the advent of modern Humanism, there has been a growing number of people who do and did, in fact, label themselves as Humanists. The list of notables within the Humanist community is quite long and impressive. I am providing you with a short list of famous modern Humanists to give you an idea of who all we are. Please realize that this list is in no way exhaustive. I just picked a few in each category so that you would understand the extent to which we Humanists play an influential role in our societies and cultures. If you do not know someone on this list, please look them up.

Scientists

Albert Einstein, physicist, was a board member of the First Humanist Society of New York and a member of the American Humanist Association.

Carl Sagan, astronomer, was a member of the American Humanist Association and received the Humanist of the Year award in 1981. He was also named Humanist Laureate for the International Academy of Humanism.

B.F. Skinner, psychologist, was Humanist of the Year in 1972 and was a signer of Humanist Manifesto II.

Francis Crick and James Watson, biochemists, were both named Humanist Laureates by the International Academy of Humanism.

Linus Pauling, chemist, was Humanist of the Year in 1961.

Jonas Salk, medical researcher, won that honor in 1976.

Writers

Isaac Asimov served as honorary president of the American Humanist Association from 1985 until his death in 1992. He was named Humanist of the Year in 1984.

Arthur C. Clarke was a distinguished supporter of the British Humanist Association and was named a Humanist Laureate by the International Academy of Humanism.

Kurt Vonnegut was the honorary president of the American Humanist Association from 1992 until his death in 2007. He was a signer of Humanist Manifesto III, *Humanism and Its Aspirations* and was named Humanist of the Year in 1992.

Gore Vidal was an honorary president of the American Humanist Association.

Joyce Carol Oates was named Humanist of the Year in 2007 by the American Humanist Association.

Christopher Hitchens was a well-known and much-loved Humanist and was a Humanist Laureate of the International Academy of Humanism.

Julian Huxley was not only a founder of the first Humanist Society of New York, but he also helped found and presided over the creation of the International Humanist and Ethical Union.

Entertainers

Gene Roddenberry was a member of the American Humanist Association and is considered one of the most influential, yet unheralded Humanists of the 20th century.

Rod Serling was a member of the Unitarian Universalists and considered himself to be a naturalistic Humanist.

Comedian Steve Allen was named Humanist Laureate by the International Academy of Humanism and was the honorary chairman of the Council for Secular Humanism until his death. His archives can be found at the offices of the Council for Secular Humanism.

Joss Whedon, the creator of Buffy the Vampire Slayer and Firefly, is a Humanist. In early 2009, he gave a presentation to the Humanist Chaplaincy at Harvard about the importance of Humanism.

Björn Ulvaeus of ABBA is a member of the Swedish Humanist Association.

Peter Ustinov was named Humanist Laureate of the International Academy of Humanism.

Social Activists

Helen Caldicott, a famous anti-nuclear advocate, was the American Humanist Association's Humanist of the Year in 1982.

A. Phillip Randolph, the civil rights activist, received the American Humanist Association's Humanist of the Year award in 1970 and was a signatory to Humanist Manifesto I.

Helen Keller was a member of the American Humanist Association and was a founding member of the First Humanist Society of New York, along with Albert Einstein.

Margaret Sanger was Humanist of the Year for the American Humanist Association in 1957.

Faye Wattleton received the Humanist of the Year award in 1986.

Andrei Sakharov received the Humanist of the Year award in 1980.

CHAPTER 5

Humanist Morality Explained

Humanism is first and foremost an ethical system. One of the first organizations to promote Humanism in America was the Ethical Culture Society. It has the word ethical in its name. Seriously, we care a lot about morality and ethics.

Our goal, as Humanists, is to be good people who do good things for our fellow humans. We do not do this because of fear of punishment after we die. We do it because being a good person has benefits here and now, and because being a good person aids in our feelings of personal happiness and fulfillment, and because we would rather be happy than sad.

Humanist Ethics Are Human Ethics

What are Humanist ethics? Humanist ethics are human ethics. They are not only derived from our natural needs, wants, and desires, but they are also fairly universal. It does not matter where you go or what you believe or do not believe about gods, the universe, and everything, most humans value the same things and our ethics, as humans, are fairly standard across the globe.

If you are religious, you might ascribe this similarity of concerns to your god's divine spark within us. For the nonreligious, it is sufficient to say that we evolved to have the emotions that cause us to judge some things as inherently right and some things as inherently wrong. What matters is that the primary emotion that leads us to make these value judgments appears to be compassion.

We Really Care

Humanism is a value system that bases its morality on our feelings of human compassion. We do not apologize for that. We feel that there is no better way of making moral judgments about what is right and what is wrong than compassion. Ours is not the only system to base our morals on compassion, but we appear to be the only one who do so without the need of any other external justification.

Humanist morality is not just about saying, "Well, my compassion tells me that helping people is good and hurting people is wrong." We can also judge whether this system works by looking at the outcomes created by this system. Things are judged as being good or bad based on how we are affected, how our communities are affected, and the how the world in which we live is affected.

Humanist thinkers throughout history have found that a compassion-based morality not only benefits us as individuals as we practice compassion, but that our communities are also improved. It simply leads to better outcomes, and that is all the justification we need to adopt and adhere to such a value system.

The Down Side

This is not to say that a compassion-based ethics is perfect or easy. It is not. Even if you choose to use compassion as your moral compass, it is very hard to sort out what is moral or immoral when the needs of one person must be weighed against the needs of another.

Different people utilizing compassion as the basis for their decision-making will often come to drastically different decisions about what is moral and what is not. The abortion debate is a prime example of this. Pretty much everyone is basing his or her opinion on compassion. Whether we primarily feel compassion for the unborn child or for the mother or for both determines how we feel about this issue.

Situational Ethics

Humanists consider our morality to be situational. We recognize that it does not matter how good any given rule is; there will always be instances when that rule should be broken in order to do the right and moral thing. Situational ethics are contrasted with absolute ethics, which hold that there are no situations that ever arise where our values are in conflict with one another, so there is never a situation where it might be considered ethical to abandon one of our values in favor of another.

The typical hypothetical example given when discussing the concept of situational ethics is when you are asked to consider whether it is okay to kill one person in order to save the lives of thousands or millions of people. Almost every human on the planet responds to this hypothetical by saying that it is moral to kill one to save thousands, but that we would rather not be put in a situation to have to make that decision. Because of this, Humanists acknowledge that all human ethics are situational, whether they are recognized as situational or not.

Adherents to absolute ethical systems scoff at this example saying such situations never actually arise in real life. Yet, they do. The killing of Osama Bin Laden by the United States is a perfect real-life example of the "kill one to save others" moral dilemma. Whether you agree with the killing of Bin Laden or not, this real-life moral dilemma required us all to consider which of our values to invoke in this particular situation. In the real world, situations do arise where our ethical system is inadequate, and we have to use our own *judgment*. Very few of us enjoyed thinking through this dilemma at all because there was no absolutely right answer. Situational ethics are the human norm, whether we like it or not.

It Takes Some Effort

While I do not want to pass judgment on the Bin Laden affair, I do want to point out that no matter how good your moral values are, you need to be prepared to make ethical and moral decisions when what is right and what is wrong is not clear. In other words, you need a moral framework for dealing with the exceptions to your normal rules of morality. Humanists solve these exceptions by trying to figure out what will do the most good and the least harm. This does require you to think and do your research.

No one said moral reasoning was easy. To be a truly moral person, you must be willing to put some effort into thinking well. This is why, Humanists consider education and critical thinking skills to be so important to moral development.

On Being Good

As for being a good person: it is not enough to want to do good. You can only be a good person by doing good things. What is the value of your professed morals if you do not put them into action? For a Humanist, a failure to act according to your moral values is a failure in your morality.

This might seem like we are highly judgmental people, but actually our focus on morality is a personal practice. This is not about preaching to others how they should behave. It is about reminding ourselves how *we* ought to behave. It is what *we* aspire to as individuals.

Humanist morality is first and foremost a personal choice. It is what we expect from ourselves that defines us as Humanists. We know that, when we adhere to our morals, we feel better and are able to achieve good things, not only for ourselves, but for others as well. When we fail to live up to our own high moral standards, we understand that we are diminished as a result.

We Humanists expect a lot from ourselves when it comes to our own personal behavior. If we mess up, which everyone does occasionally, we know that, unless we take responsibility for our actions and actively work to fix things, our guilt will gnaw away at us. It is not enough for us to say we are sorry. We actually make an effort to not make that same mistake again.

Judge Not Lest You Be Judged

Granted, while our morality is mostly focused on how we as Humanists choose to behave, that does not mean we are not going to judge the behavior of others. We have to. In our lives, we all come across people who are not nice, and who are not ethical. If we choose not to judge others, we will be unable to keep ourselves and others safe from unscrupulous individuals, and that will make it harder for us to navigate successfully through life. We must have some way of judging whether people are treating us ethically or not.

This leads to the reason why I think Humanism is so great. We judge people based on how they actually act!

It is amazing this is still considered a radical idea. We are not concerned with how people look, what their skin color is, how they did their hair, how rich they are, or even what they profess to believe. We care about how they act. We have found that judging people as individuals based on how they act and not on some other arbitrary accident of birth or social grouping gives us a really good indication of how they will act in the future!

By judging people on how they actually act, we are better able to navigate the maze of life. The advantage this gives us is so great: we dedicate a lot of our time to figuring out how to overcome and rethink our biases and bigotries. I encourage everyone to give it a try and see how it turns out for you.

When it comes to morality, Humanism is not concerned with talking a good talk. You actually have to walk the good walk to be considered an ethical person. If you fail, we will not tell you that you are going to hell. We will simply choose to avoid you in the future.

Your actions have consequences; so, choose your actions wisely. If you choose not to be an ethical person, that is your business, and you are the one who will deal with the consequences of that choice. Just know that the rest of us will be doing our best to steer clear of you.

Why We Reject Supernaturalism and Religious Approaches to Morality

Our lack of reliance on religion and supernatural beliefs is actually a huge part of the reason why we feel it is so important to be a moral person in the first place. If this is the only life we get, and it turns out that there are no gods, then how we behave toward each other here and now matters greatly. In fact, it is everything.

> *To act well, we must take responsibility for ourselves and others, not for the sake of preferential treatment in any afterlife (even if we believed in it, that motivation wouldn't make our actions good!), but because the best we can do is to live this life as brilliantly as we can. That means helping others in community, advancing society, and flourishing at whatever we do best.*
>
> —from the International Humanistic and Ethical Union (IHEU) Minimum statement on Humanism

The emphasis of many religions on an afterlife takes our focus away from the here and now. Instead of thinking about how we can help each other right now, the focus becomes how to do the will of unknowable gods. Instead of thinking about the immediate consequences of our actions, we are told to only think about the consequences in a potential afterlife that may or may not come.

Instead of seeking forgiveness from our fellow humans, we are told we only need to seek the forgiveness from a god we have never met, never seen, and of whom we have no direct knowledge.

Further, while most religions encourage us to be moral, their tendency toward dogmatism can hinder moral development. There are many studies that back that up. See Israel Wahlman's study on dogmatism and moral development for an example (https://tandfonline.com/doi/abs/10.1080/00223980.1981.9915257).

Put simply and bluntly, we Humanists think that there are better ways to teach morality than religion.

It Is a Radical Idea

The other problem Humanists have with religion is that certain forms or beliefs do not promote compassion-based ethics at all. While most people consider compassion-based ethics to be, well, basic, even going so far as to ascribe this sort of ethics to their religion, some devout believers do not. It does not matter what the religion is; devout individuals who prefer an absolute ethic based on their god's will often reject compassion outright. In this framework, compassion is considered irrelevant because, to them, it is pretty clear that whatever their god is, it's will involves a certain amount of suffering, and so, we cannot judge something as good or bad based on compassion.

While this disagreement on what the proper basis for morality is does not bother Humanists much, it matters tremendously to people who hold an absolutist non-compassion-based ethic. Believe it or not, dogmatic religious leaders see our unapologetic adherence to a compassion-based situational ethic as the most radical aspect of our philosophy.

The most radical aspect of the Humanist approach is our use of compassion as our ethical foundation. The great humanist Robert Ingersoll once spoke about wielding compassion as a sword. We are unapologetic about our use of compassion.

CHAPTER 6

I Think, Therefore I am

Humanism is not just a philosophy; it is an overall approach to living a happy and fulfilling life. One part of this approach is our adherence to compassion-based ethical values. The other part is how we think through problems. This is the other main reason we reject supernaturalism. We feel it interferes with and hinders effective problem-solving.

We Humanists are not concerned so much with what people think about as much as we are with how people think. Or specifically, how well people think. And yes, thinking well is a discipline that requires effort.

As with Humanist morality, we consider critical thinking first and foremost to be a personal practice. Something *we* aspire to. We encourage others to practice critical thinking skills simply because of how much better your thinking, and therefore your problem-solving is when you employ these techniques. Just as with morality, if you choose to think differently, that's fine too. We all have to live with the consequences of our choices.

Reality Matters

When it comes to thinking through our problems, Humanists are very much concerned with discerning, as much as possible, the real cause of our difficulties. We know that the closer our understanding of a problem is to the actual reality of what is causing it, the better our solutions will be.

Reality matters. Understanding the difference between what is real and what you imagine to be real determines whether you will be able to solve your problem, or whether you will instead spin your wheels and possibly make your problem worse.

For instance, if you have a field that needs water, and you think it is not raining because your god is mad at you, your solution to that problem is going to be to try to appease your god. This is traditionally done through some sort of sacrifice or ritual prayer. It is a supernatural approach to problem-solving.

If, on the other hand, by using critical thinking, science, and logic, you determine that it is not raining because of weather patterns beyond your control, you are more likely to look for alternatives to your problem and perhaps, figure out a way to irrigate your field instead. Using science and personal responsibility to solve a problem is the humanistic approach to problem-solving.

While this example is obvious to pretty much everyone with even the slightest bit of education, the power of this reality-based approach manifests in areas where the boundaries between what is known and what is not known are less clear.

Critical Thinking

In order to better determine what is real versus what is imagined, Humanists employ a variety of critical thinking skills. Our goal is to best determine what is real and true, so we are constantly testing our own thinking. We are skeptical of claims until they are proven. We apply the rules of logic to make sure we are not coming to any false conclusions. We prefer objective knowledge to subjective knowledge. Above all, we practice Freethought as a way to ensure that we challenge our own assumptions as rigorously as we challenge the assumptions of others.

Skepticism

This first critical thinking skill is to be skeptical. Many people think of skepticism as a negative practice; Humanists think of it as a very positive one. We know there is an objective truth out there, and that we have the ability to figure out what that is. We are not willing to allow ourselves to put our trust into something or someone just because what they are selling sounds good. We want to know if it actually works before we lay our money down.

When we are searching for a solution to a problem, we research all our options. When we come across someone who says they have a solution, we apply a healthy dose of skepticism and research their claims. What do their critics think of their work? Do they have any testable and verifiable science to back up their claims? These are all reasonable questions to ask of someone who is claiming that they can solve our problems. If they cannot answer them to our satisfaction, we look elsewhere. Again, this is not a negative process unless you are invested in a solution that has not been proven to work because you are either the person selling it or the person buying it.

Logic and Science

When evaluating claims, Humanists rely on the twin disciplines of logic and science. Logic helps us determine whether our own or someone else's arguments in support of a claim are valid. Science helps us determine whether the premises in the argument are even true in the first place.

We consider these skills to be useful in every aspect of our lives. From what shampoo we buy to the food we choose to eat to what politicians we choose to vote for. All around us people are making claims, and it benefits us to know whether those claims are both logical and scientifically sound.

Freethought

Freethought is considered a central discipline for Humanist thought because your ability to think critically is limited without it. The term Freethought is often used interchangeably with *critical thinking* and that is because they both use the same skill set. But, I like to treat Freethought as its own process because at the heart of Freethinking is the willingness to challenge your own assumptions. This is perhaps the hardest aspect of thinking critically.

Freethinkers refuses to limit their thinking. We reject as arbitrary all social taboos, accepted wisdom, and biases, and we challenge ourselves to think beyond those limitations to determine whether they are valid or not. Again, our goal is to discern what is true and what is real. If we limit ourselves to what is known and accepted, and if we are not willing to challenge our own assumptions and biases, we will never be able to solve our most intractable problems.

CHAPTER 7

Cockeyed Optimism

The last thing you should know about Humanism is that it is optimistic. In fact, we Humanists can seem a bit cockeyed at times. That is just an illusion though because we Humanists do actively and rigorously engage in critical thinking, and so are often a bit more aware of what is possible than others might realize.

One of the main reasons we encourage optimism in ourselves and in others is because we know that optimism is the key to our motivation to act. Without a positive belief that we can make a difference, we have no impetus to try. Unless we act, we will continue to be mired in the current status quo. I am not sure about your life, but mine always seems to be in need of improvement.

So, let us look at the various aspects of how Humanists use and cultivate optimism.

I Can Do Anything You Can Do Better

Humanists are, generally speaking, unwilling to accept the status quo if the status quo involves suffering of any kind. We do not normally talk about sin, but if there is a sin in this life, it surely involves suffering unnecessarily. As Albert Camus once said,

> *Perhaps we cannot prevent this world from being a world in which children are tortured. But we can reduce the number of tortured children. And if you don't help us, who else in the world can help us do this?*
>
> —Albert Camus, The Unbeliever and the Christians

As far as we Humanists are concerned, suffering is not noble, and we rarely learn anything useful from it. It is painful, and we would like to avoid it as much as possible.

For the record, we do not just feel that way about our own suffering. We feel that way about others' as well. In fact, our own misery is in many ways easier to tolerate because it is happening to us. Watching others endure hardship is virtually intolerable.

Because we do not like to see harm come to others, and we do not like to experience unnecessary pain ourselves, we are always looking for ways in which we can improve what we are doing and make life better for everyone. This is the heart of Epicurean reasoning.

Whatever it is we are doing now, we are sure there is a better, more effective, and efficient way to do it. Yes, we may be overly optimistic. But, it is the refusal to accept the status quo and a belief that we can do better that drives innovation. All innovation.

If you do not believe you can do better, there is no reason to try. Believe you can and you pretty much have the responsibility to make an effort. This may be the reason why so many Nobel Laureates are professed Humanists. Even though there are not very many of us in society, we are so active in pushing for innovation and progress that our influence greatly outweighs our numbers.

The Future Is so Bright, I've Got to Wear Shades

The second important aspect of our optimism is our focus on the future. Humanists are almost all futurists. We enjoy thinking about what the future may be like. We enjoy thinking that there may come a time when equality is a reality; when disease and illness are things of the past; when we are able to live together in peace and harmony with goodwill toward all. And of course, we can envision a time when we are living in a sustainable way in harmony with nature.

Even though we can imagine such a future, that does not mean we think it would be easy to get there or that it is even possible to achieve. Though we may, at times, have our heads in the clouds, Humanism is an incredibly pragmatic philosophy. We understand the difference between having an ideal you are aiming for and what you might realistically achieve. We just feel that it is better to have an ideal to work toward than to abandon the present to despair.

We are willing to work toward our goals incrementally, one step at a time. Baby steps if that is what it takes, as long as we keep pushing toward that ideal future. Yes, it takes time. Yes, it requires attitudes to change. But, look at all we have accomplished so far:

Slavery is now considered morally wrong pretty much everywhere.

Skin color is no longer a socially acceptable way to judge people.

Women are not only able to vote and own property, they can also work and enter into any field of endeavor they want (in many countries—though there is clearly still more work to do in this area).

Education is now considered a universal right for all children everywhere (though again—not always for female children).

The death penalty has been abolished in most countries.

Torture is now considered a crime against humanity.

Despite all the setbacks and problems, the world community is working together on a wide variety of projects that would have been unimaginable just a couple of decades ago.

The concept of Human Rights, just 50 years old, is now an accepted legal doctrine and something people everywhere demand for themselves.

And that is just a few of the advances in the social arena. When we look at the advances in medicine and science, the list of achievements is astonishing. And, they are all fairly recent. From our perspective, the future is indeed bright.

Stand and Deliver

The most powerful aspect of the Humanist philosophy is that it encourages us to take responsibility for our lives and for the lives of those around us. We alone are responsible to make things better. To re-quote Camus, If we don't, who will?

The great thing about responsibility is that, once you embrace it, you are empowered to act. By acting, you inspire others to take responsibility as well. The great lesson of Humanism is that you do not need everyone. Just a few committed people are enough to create societal change on a global scale.

Humanism is a progressive philosophy of life that, without supernaturalism, affirms our ability and responsibility to lead ethical lives of personal fulfillment that aspire to the greater good of humanity. It is a commitment to act according to our highest ideals and to work toward the betterment of humanity. It is an individual's commitment to stand and deliver on the promise of the future.

While we realize we may not be able achieve our ideal future, Humanists are committed to getting as close to that ideal as possible. If you will not help us, who will?

CHAPTER 8

Resources

There are organizations and a wide variety of resources that can help you explore the philosophy of Humanism further. I also encourage you to check out my other books and online resources I have made available at www.jen-hancock.com.

Online Resources

These resources can be found on the Web.

Humanist Manifesto III, published in 2003 by the American Humanist Association: http://americanhumanist.org/Who_We_Are/About_Humanism/Humanist_Manifesto_III

Essays in Humanism, a journal published by the American Humanist Association: http://essaysinhumanism.org/

The Genesis of a Humanist Manifesto by Edwin H Wilson: http://infidels.org/library/modern/edwin_wilson/manifesto/index.html

Books published by the Humanist Press: http://evolvefish.com/fish/HumanistPress.html

Humanist books from Prometheus Books: http://prometheusbooks.com/index.php?main_page=index&cPath=35_31

More online essays from the American Humanist Association: http://americanhumanist.org/Who_We_Are/About_Humanism

The Humanist Tradition from the British Humanist Association: http://humanism.org.uk/humanism/humanist-tradition

Introduction to Humanism video series by Jennifer Hancock: http://youtube.com/playlist?list=PL926B6F22CBF88997

Humanist Heritage provides background on the history of Humanism in the UK: http://humanistheritage.org.uk/

Books

Here are some books on Humanism you might find interesting. You should be able to find these books wherever books are sold.

The Way of Ethical Humanism by Gerald Larue

Humanism as the Next Step by Mary and Lloyd Morain

The Philosophy of Humanism by Corliss Lamont

Freethinkers: A history of American Secularism by Susan Jacoby

Good Without God by Greg Epstein

Humanism and Democratic Criticism by Edward Said

The Humanist Approach to Happiness: Practical Wisdom by Jennifer Hancock

Humanism for Parents by Sean Curley

Raising Freethinkers by Dale McGowan

Charities

Humanists are very philanthropic-minded. It is part of our philosophy that we should try to help make the world a better place. Here are some Humanist charities that raise money to aid people in disasters and for other causes. All in the name of Humanism.

Humanist Charities run by the American Humanist Association: http://humanistcharities.org/

Foundation Beyond Belief: http://foundationbeyondbelief.org/

Humanist Kiva Lending Group: http://kiva.org/team/humanist

Organizations

If you are looking for a local Humanist group, please check out the national and international organizations to find a group in your area.

The International Humanist and Ethical Union: http://iheu.org/ has a list of organizations by country.

The British Humanist Association: http://humanism.org.uk/home

The American Humanist Association: http://americanhumanist.org/

There are also several humanistic groups available. For instance:

The American Ethical Union: http://aeu.org/

The Society for Humanistic Judaism: http://shj.org/

The Center for Inquiry, which hosts the Council for Secular Humanism: http://centerforinquiry.net/

The HUUmanists, Humanists within the UUA: http://huumanists.org/

PART II

Applying Humanism to the World of Business

How to be successful, happy, and ethical in the world of business.

CHAPTER 1

Why Apply Humanism to Business?

Humanistic business management is a relatively new buzzword in business. It represents the application of the Humanist philosophy to the business of business.

The first part of this book provided an overview of the Humanist philosophy. This part will discuss how it can be applied to business and why it is so effective when you do so.

You do not need to be a Humanist to utilize these methods. As with any philosophic approach, take what works for you and ignore the stuff that does not. No one is going to test you on this unless you are reading this book for a class. It is up to you to decide what to take, if anything, from this approach. What I will tell you is that Humanists are some of the most influential people in our society, and they are usually very successful in life.

This part of the book will help answer the questions: "Why is Humanism suddenly so popular? More importantly, how can we apply it to our businesses and other endeavors?"

Humanism 101: A Recap

According to the American Humanist Association, Humanism is a progressive philosophy of life that, without supernaturalism, affirms our ability and responsibility to lead ethical lives of personal fulfillment that aspire to the greater good of humanity. In plain English, that means—life your life to the fullest, love other people, and try to leave the world a better place.

Another way to think about Humanism is to think of it as a commitment that you make to yourself to be a good person. As the great Kurt

Vonnegut once said, "I am a Humanist which means in part that I have tried to behave decently without expectation of reward or punishment after I am dead."

Like Mr. Vonnegut, I am a Humanist because I have made a commitment to myself to be the best most ethical person I can be. Why? Because that is the sort of person I want to be. It benefits me in the here and now to be a good person. Self-identifying as a Humanist helps remind me that I need to actively live up to my ideals. I desire to live well and to help create a society in which everyone can flourish.

Humanism is a philosophy of life, but it is so much more than that. It impacts how you choose to look at the world and interact with it. It is about being ethical, compassionate, honest, and responsible. It is as concerned with how well you think through your problems as it is about what you value. This is why, it is such a powerful philosophy and why its application to all that you do yields such tremendous results.

Main Principles

There are several aspects of the philosophy that are relevant to business, and it is these aspects I will be discussing in detail.

The principles I will be discussing in this book include:

- A compassion-based ethic
- Reality-based pragmatic problem-solving
- Respect for the dignity and worth of each human
- Personal and social responsibility
- Living a fulfilling life

Humanistic Versus Humanist

A reminder about nomenclature. I am a Humanist, which means, I have adopted all aspects of the philosophy. If you do as well, you are probably a Humanist too. However, there are elements of the philosophy and approach that some people do not agree with, even though they agree with most of it.

Humanism is an ethical philosophy that is as much concerned about ethics as it is with problem-solving and compassion. Most people agree with humanistic ethics, our compassion, and humanistic problem-solving. The one aspect of Humanism that gives people pause is usually our rejection of the supernatural.

There are two areas where rejection of supernaturalism comes up: in our ethics and in our decision-making. The good news is that even if you disagree with us on metaphysical matters, it will not affect your ability to apply these skills and approach to your own needs and purposes.

If, as you are reading through the book, you find yourself disagreeing with my Humanist rejection of supernaturalism, but agree with everything else, you are taking a humanistic approach, which, while not fully Humanist, does include some of the most important aspects of the philosophy. Taking a hybrid approach to the philosophy really is OK. In fact, it is incredibly common.

For example: Consider the secular nature of Humanist ethics. Humanist ethics are rational ethics, and they do contrast with religious ethics. Religious ethics tend to be about the consequences of your behavior in an afterlife. Rational ethics are about what the consequences to your behavior are in the here and now. For most people, their religious ethics are the same as their rational ethics, and there is no conflict. They simply have a variety of reasons why something is considered good or bad. To translate this for you: a Humanist is concerned solely with the consequences of your actions in the here and now. A humanistic person is probably concerned with both the here and now and with an afterlife.

In the area of problem-solving, Humanists adhere to reality-based decision-making, and we reject appeals for supernatural intervention as ineffective and unreliable. The way I normally describe this is that, if you have a field that needs water, you can pray for rain, irrigate your field, or both irrigate and pray. Praying is obviously a supernatural approach to solving the problem. Irrigating the field is a pragmatic approach. Most people, regardless of belief, adopt a pragmatic approach to problem-solving because it provides a more reliable solution to our problems. For instance, if you pray for rain, you may or may not get water on your field. If you irrigate your field, you will definitely get water on your field. The Humanist approach is to irrigate the field. The humanistic approach is to both irrigate the field and pray for rain. These both contrast with a strictly religious approach, which is to just pray and hope for the best.

The reason people choose a Humanist or humanistic approach to problem-solving is because it is considered more reliable, and therefore, more effective than the alternatives.

Whether you personally choose a humanist, humanistic, or religious approach to solving your problems is up to you. My job in this book is to teach you the humanist approach so that you can at least make an informed decision.

The Benefits of a Humanistic Approach

What are the benefits of taking a humanistic approach to your life and to your business? While there are no guarantees in life, if you can change the odds in your favor, you give yourself an advantage that other people do not have. If you can solve your problems effectively and ethically, you are going to be more successful. If you can manage to actively live by your ethics, you are going to find more satisfaction in your life and in your work than if you abandon them to expediency. Additionally, because a humanistic approach is based on compassion for others, you are going to find that your interpersonal relationships are deeper and more satisfying as well.

In other words, adopting a humanistic approach should help you think better, have better relationships, and feel more fulfilled.

What this does not mean is that you are going to succeed at everything you try to do. You will not. It also does not mean that you will not encounter adversity, you will. You will not be happy all the time either. No one is.

All this approach allows you to do is help you deal with life's adversities more effectively and to make better decisions that have a greater likelihood of success than alternative methods. At the end of the day, this is a better guarantee of success than wishful thinking, and it is, therefore, preferable to methods that promise quick fixes and hollow assurances that do not deliver on those promises and blame you for not thinking enough positive thoughts.

Warning: The Humanist or humanistic approach is hard work, which is why not everyone chooses it. The rewards for doing the hard work required are increased levels of satisfaction in life, higher levels of well-being, and more effective solutions for your business.

Applied Humanism

How do I know that Humanism, when it gets applied to human endeavors, yields such good results? Let us look at the evidence.

While Humanism is a personal philosophy of choice, there are several fields that have already adopted and integrated a humanistic approach and their successes are well known.

Humanistic Psychology

The first example I am going to provide is that of humanistic psychology. The Association for Humanistic Psychology was founded in 1962 by Humanists Abraham Maslow, Carl Rogers, and others. Their goal was to use psychology to *enhance the quality of human experience* for everyone. The principles that humanistic psychology emphasized were human dignity and worth, individual freedom and responsibility, compassion for everyone, and ethical relationships.

To understand the impact this movement has had on psychology, and as a result, on our society, you need to understand what psychiatric care was like before humanistic psychology. It was not that long ago that mentally ill individuals and people with various brain disorders and even people who were developmentally disabled were simply locked away from the rest of society. Very little effort was made to help these people. They were store-housed away from the rest of us. The idea that they could be integrated into society or that they were, in fact, valuable members of our society who had every right to live their lives to their fullest potential despite their differently abled abilities, was simply not something anyone even considered. It is no surprise to find that some of the first advocates for disabled rights were Humanists. Helen Keller, for instance, helped found the First Humanist Society of New York along with Julian Huxley.

We also need to remember that it was not that long ago that people with schizophrenia, epilepsy, or other mental disorders were treated for demonic possession. Exorcisms were performed on people, and in some cases, still are. We can recognize this now as a supernatural approach to solving what is actually a natural neurological problem. Once we started treating these disorders as a natural neurological problem as opposed to a supernatural or spiritual one, we were able to find solutions for them that actually work quite well and allow individuals with these disorders to live life fully as valued members of society.

There is no question that psychiatric care became more effective and more compassionate once a humanistic approach to psychology was taken. In fact, it has been so successful that they do not even talk about humanistic psychology as something independent of general psychology anymore. Humanistic psychology has proven itself to be so successful at both treating problems and at helping people flourish that it is now just called psychology.

Other Humanistic Associations

In addition to the Association of Humanistic Psychology, there are also associations for humanistic medicine, the Gold Humanist Society is well known in medical schools. There are humanistic nursing associations, humanistic sociology associations, and humanistic anthropology associations.

The humanistic approach is so dynamic and flexible that it not only helps individuals lead happy and fulfilling lives, it can be applied with equally good results to any area of human endeavor without changing the basic principles at work.

Humanistic Business Management

Let us talk about how humanism can be applied to business. Perhaps the best way to do this is to talk about the principles that make up the philosophy itself so that you can see how they are applied.

The principle purpose of humanism is to:

- Be the best most ethical person you can be
- Treat everyone you interact with and meet with dignity and compassion

- Make the focus on your work helping others and improving life for everyone on the planet
- Be responsible
- Do the best you can in all that you do

The Humanistic Management Network lists as its objectives:

The development of a worldwide human society accepting of cultural diversity, respect for nature as the basis for living and equal rights for all people. There is an understanding that business and economics are primary drivers for any society. So how can we best focus our businesses to enhance and enrich life for everyone, and not just a select few? Humanistic business management understands that an enlightened individual accepts our interconnectedness and aims to improve society for everyone and not just themselves. By improving society, they improve the support society provides to them as well as to everyone else. In other words, humanistic business management is just another way to talk about the importance enlightened self-interest plays in our business dealings. We understand that when we are utterly self-serving materialistic beings (i.e., homo economicus) we are at our worse and that we can and should be better than that.

Humanistic business management, like all forms of Humanism, is a choice. It is a choice to conduct your business in accordance with your deeply held values. It is a choice to reject the false dichotomy that says, you either take a heartless approach to your business or you will fail. It is a choice to say that no, you will not pursue profits over people.

Humanistic business managers understand that they can both make a profit and help make the world a better place at the same time, and that by choosing this approach, they will not only help make the world a better place, they will also help themselves find fulfillment and happiness in their work and in their lives.

As I see it, there are four basic rules of humanistic business management.

1. Do no evil: Be the best most ethical person you can be.
2. Reality matters: Making good decisions requires you to know what is really going on.

3. Respect people: It is not humanistic business management if you do not care about humans.

4. It is your responsibility: You and you alone can choose how you are going to act.

CHAPTER 2

Rule #1 Do No Evil

The single most important aspect of humanistic business management is the emphasis this philosophy places on ethics.

Ethics is a system of values. It is your personal guide to deciding whether something is good, sort of good, sort of bad, or really bad. Without some guidelines to help you determine whether something is good or bad, you have no way to judge whether the decisions you are making are good or not.

Normally, in business, something is considered good if it helps you make money. In this value system, making money is considered good. Obviously, most people do not recognize this as a valid value system because if all you value is money, something is amiss. This is not to say that making money is bad; it is just that most value systems value more than just one thing, and it is the combination of values that makes up our ethical system. The critical question all ethical systems must answer is what do we value most?

As it turns out, studies of global ethics[1] indicate that most people value compassion above everything else. This means that most of us tend to judge things as good or bad based on the impact they have on real people (i.e., us). In a compassionate-based ethical system, good and bad are determined as follows: if it helps someone, it is good; if it hurts, it is bad.

The problem with ethical systems is that even the simplest system like our compassion-based one requires us to balance our needs against the needs of other people. For instance, if something helps me but hurts another person; is that good or bad? A humanistic value system is one where we take the responsibility on ourselves to do the most good and the least harm to ourselves and to others.

---

[1] https://edge.org/conversation/it-seems-biology-not-religion-equals-morality

The next difficulty to address is the fact that what is good or bad is rather subjective to the individual. While you might really like something, someone else might find it really bad. For instance, you might enjoy chocolate ice cream, but if a friend of yours has a chocolate allergy, getting them a chocolate ice cream simply because you like it would not only not be very nice; it would actually be pretty cruel.

Understanding the difference between your needs and the needs of others is key to understanding and implementing ethics in your life. Ethics is not about how you should treat other people; it is actually all about how you yourself want to be treated. My guess is that you would like it people were honest with you, treated you with dignity and compassion, respected you for the individual you are, and did not lump you in with the jerks of the world just because of some perceived similarity between you and a jerk they happen to know.

You would probably also like it if people were responsible and did the things they said they were going to. If everyone behaved like this, it would make your life easier.

The question of ethics boils down to this: what is in it for you? Why should you be honest, compassionate, and responsible with the people you meet, and why should you take their needs into account? The answer is contained in the golden rule. There is a reason why pretty much every culture has a version of this. Do unto others as you would have them do unto you. If you are not willing to treat other people with dignity and compassion, you should not expect them to treat you well either.

The real reason to be a good person is because ethical, compassionate, and responsible people hate hanging out and doing business with people who are not responsible, ethical, or compassionate. The way to hang out with and do business with good people is to be a good person yourself.

If all this does not convince you to be moral, consider this. You have a self-image of yourself, and most of us want our self-image to be a good one. Being good impacts our self-esteem and our sense of self-worth. The better your self-image, the happier most people are with themselves. You know when you are living up to your ideals as a human being, and you know when you are not. I know that I do not feel very good about myself when I do not live up to my ideals. When I do, I am not only proud of myself, I feel very happy and like I am getting life right. I am the person I should be. If that is not happiness, I do not know what is.

If you want to be happy, you need to be a good person. Not being a good person might gain you some short-term advantages in the struggle for business, but you are cheating yourself out of well-earned self-esteem and your reputation as an unethical person will close off lucrative opportunities to you. To me, the tradeoff is not worth it.

(Note: I go into this concept in more detail in my six-week course, *Living Made Simpler*. If this is something you are struggling with and would like to delve into deeper learning, I encourage you to get my *Living Made Simpler* course. For more details, go to http://humanisthappiness.com.)

Compassion

A value system can be based on anything. It could be based on the value of material wealth. It could be based on your status in society. Humanism bases our value judgments for what is good or bad on compassion. We are unapologetic about that.

We base our ethics on compassion for several reasons. First, it works. The outcomes of decisions made with compassion yield better results for just about everyone involved, including ourselves. One of the main objections to a compassion-based approach is that people sometimes think that, if they are being compassionate, they are putting other people first. You are not because you should also be applying compassion to yourself. Consider this an exercise in enlightened self-interest. Being compassionate with others and yourself yields good results for everyone involved.

Another reason why Humanists choose compassion as our primary good is because there is really no other metric that make sense, which is why there is now a global movement to measure well-being, instead of wealth, as a measure of a country's economic success.[2]

Compassion is the only emotion we are almost all hard-wired to experience. Compassion really does act as a moral compass for most people (psychopathic personalities excluded). When we hurt other people, most of us feel guilt, and that is a good thing. That is our compassion at work.

---

[2] https://forbes.com/sites/joshuacohen/2018/10/15/measuring-well-being-its-more-than-gdp

The good news is that compassion is a nearly universal emotion, and it is the basis of most of the moral codes and religions on the planet for a reason. It is a very powerful emotion to feel, and it is really hard to deny when you experience it. Because of its universality, it can help us create a common moral language through which we can motivate diverse staff to make ethical decisions together.

The final reason you should consider making compassion the foundation of your moral reasoning is because feeling compassion makes you feel better. Consider this scenario. You are in a crowded shopping store and everyone is hassled. Do you approach this situation with frustration or with compassion for yourself, for the other shoppers and for the clerks who deal with it all?

Which emotion feels better in the moment? Most people are going to say they would rather feel compassion. Why? Because it feels better than frustration! Which emotion makes you feel like a good human being? Again, compassion. This is reason enough to practice compassion and make it the center of your ethics and your decision-making process.

Additionally, as we are talking about how this applies to business, consider the impact responding with compassion will have on the clerks involved in our crowded store. Speaking as a former store clerk, I can attest to the fact that crowded stores can be quite stressful, and that the impulse is to join the crowd in their frenzied rush. Trying to help everyone simultaneously helps no one.

I was taught a valuable lesson about how to approach these stressful crowds by one of my early managers. Whenever we had a rush, he would actually slow down and make sure to give the customer directly in front of him his full attention. It was as if the line did not exist. Believe it or not, this made things go quicker. The main reason things went more smoothly was because he made fewer mistakes, which meant less work correcting mistakes and happier customers. Additionally, because his customers did not feel like they were being short-changed for attention, he had fewer lingerers, or customers who refuse to finish their transaction because they do not feel satisfied with how much attention was paid to them.

This is a very real phenomenon that can really exacerbate a crowded sales floor. The way to fix it is to be compassionate with your customers and give them the attention they deserve. My former manager knew this, and that is why when he slowed down intentionally, things went more quickly for everyone with fewer hassles.

For the few truly frazzled customers who blew their tops, he would handle them compassionately as well. The best thing he or anyone can do for an upset customer is to handle their transaction in a calm, professional, effective manner and to give them your full compassionate attention, even if they are being jerks.

This brings me to the final reason why a compassion-based ethics is superior to the alternatives. When I am able to actively be compassionate with the jerks of the world, I feel like I am at my best. I also know how not living up to my ideals feels. I do not know anyone who has not experienced frustration in a store and who has not felt bad about how they handled their frustration. In those few instances when you are able to respond to stressful situations with compassion, you know you are a good human being. That is a feeling that cannot be bought.

Now, imagine if you had that feeling of knowing you are a good person almost all of the time, and that it permeated every aspect of your life, including your work and your business? Isn't that the definition of well-being?

The question we all need to ask ourselves, because being compassionate has so many benefits to us here and now, is how we can be more actively compassionate, including in those experiences we find the most frustrating. The answer is to make a commitment to yourself to be actively compassionate and to remind yourself of your commitment on an ongoing basis so that when you get frustrated, you will remind yourself to take the high road. This is why people choose to take a humanistic approach to every aspect of their lives.

What About Money?

Choosing to make being compassionate a priority does not mean that you do not value other things, like making money and making a living. The key is to figure out how to make money and still conduct your business in an ethically compassionate way. Taking a compassionate approach only means you are not willing to make money by causing someone else harm. You can still make a lot of money operating in a compassionate way.

Your goal as a humanistic business manager is to weigh your business opportunities not solely on the potential return on investment, but also by how much good or harm you will be causing as a result of engaging in this business.

The idea that you either make money or you help people is what is known as a false dichotomy. You have other options. A humanistic business manager is the one who looks for those other options. Or, in buzz words terms, a humanistic business manager is the one who makes an effort to find a win–win scenario.

What you are looking for are opportunities that will help people, will not cause any harm, and that will also provide you with a good potential return on investment.

Additionally, when you are solving problems in the course of your business, a humanistic business manager will consider a variety of methods of solving the problem and will choose the one that will solve the problem effectively and help you make money all while doing the most good for humanity, and without causing any unnecessary harm.

Lazy business people like to fall back on the false belief that the harm they cause is necessary for their business as a way to absolve themselves of the guilt they are feeling for doing something they know is wrong.

This manifests in business in a variety of ways, and we all know the stories. The common element in all of them is greed and a dehumanizing of the customer so that the customer is not considered an individual worthy of dignity and compassion.

For instance, some businesses sell products they know their customers do not need and cannot really afford. Others know that their products are designed to fail so that the customer will have to pay for service. Some intentionally manipulate the market so that their products are grossly overpriced, despite the harm these manipulations cause to real people. The Enron scandal in 2001 was an example of this sort of unethical business practice where they literally shut off the electricity to the state of California to manipulate energy prices and joked about it.

Some companies take shortcuts knowing that they are taking a safety risk that might turn out badly. This is what happened at BP's Deep-Water Horizon facility in 2010. Others sell products they know will harm their customers figuring that, if their customers are stupid enough to buy the product, then they deserve to have their money taken.

Do not allow yourself to ever consider your customers as worthy of your scorn. Do not ever dehumanize them as a way to rationalize *your* bad behavior. Do not allow yourself to make mistakes that may cost an employee or your customers their lives. Make the effort to find a business solution that will benefit everyone, including your bank account.

Those solutions are out there. Be committed to finding them and value your compassion for others more than you do greed.

I am Reviewing the Situation

The toughest aspect of being a good person is that it takes a bit of effort. If it was easy to make the right decisions, you would not need a book like this one. The truth is that ethical situations are rarely cut and dried, and we often find ourselves facing morally difficult problems. We do have to weigh the needs of one group of people and the harm we might cause them off the needs of another group of people who might be benefited if we go ahead with our plans. No one likes having to make these sorts of hard decisions. But, that is the purpose of ethics. It is not about choosing between good and evil. It is about figuring out the best solution when the situation is not ideal. Sometimes, your only choice is between the greater of two goods or the lesser of two evils.

The humanistic approach is to accept the responsibility of applying your ethics to the real-world situations you find yourself in, regardless of how difficult they are. If you are not willing to take on that responsibility or you are not willing to do the hard thinking required to make sure your decisions do the most good and the least harm, then you probably should not be in a leadership position at all.

Humanistic business managers embrace the responsibility that ethical decision-making requires and put a lot of effort into making sure their moral reasoning is strong. The good news is that, far from being a burden, accepting and embracing your responsibilities as a good human being is empowering and adds tremendously to your sense of self-worth and motivation.

Not only will you be making better decisions if you decide to take on the responsibility to do the work required to make sure your decisions are good ones, you will also benefit from the emotional satisfaction that you gain from being responsible to your moral values. People who chose ethics as their primary motivation never lack for motivation.

And, if all that was not enough, your decisions will be better too. Better decisions result in more success.

What do you need to know to make good moral decisions?

1. Understand that you do indeed have to think
2. Commit to learning how to think well
3. Be humble enough to correct your mistakes

Let us take each of these in turn.

I Think, Therefore I Am

Humanist ethics are situational ethics, which means there are no hard-and-fast-rules to our ethics. Instead, we have a set of principles and values that need to be considered and weighed against one another to determine the best and most moral outcome for any given situation.

A lot of people struggle with situational ethics. They want a hard and fast absolute rule that they can apply to whatever situation they find themselves in because that requires less intellectual work. They just apply the rule and go on and hope for the best.

The problem with absolute ethics is that they are not realistic because there will always be situations where the rules need to be broken to do the right thing and they are not flexible, so they are limited to the ideal situations for which the rule was created in the first place. We do not live in an ideal world. The world we live in is constantly changing. As a result, it does not matter how good the rule is; there will always be situations where an exception has to be made.

For example: when my son was four, I found him with a handful of pennies in his mouth, so I made a new rule. If it is not food, it does not belong in your mouth. This is a simple rule very few people will disagree with. The problem, as my sister so kindly pointed out, is that toothbrushes are not food, yet they belong in your mouth. Same with toothpaste.

It does not matter how obvious a rule is, there will always be exceptions to it. For instance, thou shalt not kill is a pretty universally accepted rule. But … there are always going to be situations that put our values in conflict with themselves. For instance, is it OK to kill one person to save the lives of others? This is the moral dilemma behind the death penalty. It was the moral dilemma President Obama had to decide when he chose to kill Osama Bin Laden.

I am not writing this to get you to consider whether the death penalty is moral or not or to litigate Obama's decision. I am only using these as examples to make the point, you need a moral system that is robust enough to help you sort through the moral dilemmas that present themselves in real life. Not idealized life.

This means you need a moral system that is grounded in principle values. You need to be prepared to apply those values to situations that are not cut and dry. Finally, you need to learn how to think well so that you can be sure your moral reasoning is as strong as it can be. In order to be truly moral, you do need to know how to think.

Critical Thinking 101

This brings us to the topic of critical thinking. There are two aspects to critical thinking that help you apply your moral values to your everyday life. The first is that learning how to think well will help you think more effectively about moral problems. The second thing is that the quality of your moral reasoning is entirely dependent on whether what you think you know is even so. If you are basing your moral reasoning on a lie, your moral reasoning will be flawed.

Additionally, when solving a problem ethically and effectively, you need to know what is actually causing the problem, as opposed to what you assume is causing the problem. You need to be able to consider alternative solutions to the problem and to be able to pick the solution that has the best chance of success and that will do the most good and the least harm in the process. You cannot do any of that well unless you know how to think well.

The next chapter will delve into critical thinking in more details; for now, understand that thinking critically is important to humanistic business management for two reasons: your moral reasoning is limited by your ability to think responsibly and the more you are able to think critically and clearly, the better your problem-solving will be. So yes, you do need to commit to the life-long study of learning how to think.

Humble Pie Tastes Better than You Think

The third part of moral reasoning is to understand that no one is perfect. Everyone makes mistakes. To be a moral person, you need to be willing to admit you made a mistake and to correct your mistakes as soon as possible.

I realize a lot of people have a really hard time admitting they were wrong or that they did something wrong. We are all afraid to face the fact we screwed up because accepting that we did does not feel all that good.

To get yourself over this hurdle, always remember, the only thing worse than being wrong is continuing to be wrong once it has been pointed out to you. Do not double down on your mistakes. That only makes matters worse for yourself and for the people your actions are affecting.

If you truly want to be a moral person, you need to learn the joys of humility. Yes, humility is humbling, and it does not always feel good. Knowing you took responsibility for your actions does feel good. Knowing you did not pass the blame feels great. Knowing you are courageous enough to admit your mistakes and correct them feels fantastic. The added bonus is that, by taking the responsibility to fix a problem, you are fixing a problem. That means you are causing less problems for yourself and everyone else.

Fixing problems makes life easier. Ignoring your problems makes life harder. Find the courage and own up to your responsibilities. Embrace the good feelings that come with being responsible and make your life easier at the same time. Humble pie really does taste pretty good.

Why Are Things So Hard?

As we have discussed so far, the humanistic approach to ethics is to base our decisions for what is good and what is bad on compassion, and that there are no hard-and-fast rules. We must apply our ethical reasoning to the various situations we find ourselves in.

If you are in a business dealing with water resources, for instance, what might be good for one set of people (i.e., providing clean drinking water to them) might actually harm another group of people by diverting their water supply to the people you are trying to help through your business. This is a very common problem in India right now. Fights over water in Los Angeles are so legendary—the movie *Chinatown* has it as a central plot point. Wars are fought over this very problem.

If you are in the energy industry, you know that most of the choices that are made involve a tradeoff. The need to create energy versus the harm that producing that energy causes.

I could go on with examples, but you get the idea. Business decisions are almost always of the *how to do the most good while doing the least harm* variety. Small businesses are not immune from making difficult decisions either. All businesses need energy and consume resources in some fashion. Those resources come from somewhere, and someone is probably being negatively impacted by their extraction. Additionally, all businesses create waste. How we deal with that waste impacts other people.

To make matters even more complicated, we make our decisions, not in an ideal world, but in the competitive world of commerce. If you take on an extra expense to clean your effluent so as not to impact the water supply and your competitor does not, they will have an unfair cost advantage in competing with you.

Do not let the difficulty of making these decisions deter you. Do not go along and do what everyone else does if you know that doing so is causing harm. What makes a humanistically run business unique is that the managers took the time to figure out how to solve their problems in a way that results in savings for the company and a benefit to the community in which they operate. They are able to do so in large part because they were committed to doing so and because they did not accept the status quo as inevitable. In other words, if an ideal solution did not exist, they invented it.

For case studies, I recommend you purchase the book *Humanistic Management in Practice* by the Humanistic Business Network. It is a book of case studies that will help you understand the decisions humanistic business managers make that help them succeed and do good at the same time.

CHAPTER 3

Rule #2 Reality Matters

Thinking about ethics is hard. We are rarely choosing between what is good and what is bad. We are usually choosing between the lesser of two evils or the greater of two goods. To make these sorts of decisions requires us to think well.

Failure to think well results in poor decision-making. Poor decision-making results in shoddy ethics, poor performance, and problems that go unsolved and become chronic.

This is why Humanists spend so much time learning about and practicing critical thinking skills. Critical thinking is the set of skills that help you determine whether something is true, false, partially true, partially false, sometimes true, or sometimes false.

But wait, if something is true, doesn't it mean it is true? Why all the sub-categories of partially true or sometimes true? True is true? True? The reality is that sometimes things are only partially true or sometimes true and sometimes false, and reality really matters.

The effectiveness of your problem-solving is entirely dependent on whether what you think you know is even so. The closer your understanding of how things work matches up to the reality of how they actually work, the more effective you are going to be.

Let me give you a couple of real-life examples of what I am talking about.

1. Witchcraft. If you live in the west, you will probably laugh this off, but for the millions of people and children around the world who are accused of witchcraft every year, it is no laughing matter. It is a matter of life and death. If you are a farmer and your crop is failing. Is it because of a drought, or did someone put a curse on you? Your answer to this question dictates how you go about solving your problem. In areas where there is still a strong belief in witchcraft, witches are often blamed and then, some holy man goes on a witch

hunt, convinces a parent their child is a witch, and the child is either killed or ostracized from the community. It happens quite a bit in places like Nigeria, though police in places like Miami report that some immigrant populations do not understand why witchcraft is not illegal in the United States. It is a tricky problem for the police because, if they do not act, the community might go *vigilante* and that never ends well.

2. Imagine you have epilepsy. Is that caused by a chemical imbalance in the brain? Or, is it caused by demonic possession? If you live in the west, you probably discount the supernatural scenario as unrealistic. However, the *Arab News* recently was compelled to report that epilepsy is not caused by Jinns, and that doing exorcisms is not likely to cure the problem. This was a public service report to encourage people to seek medical help instead of going to an exorcist.

These are two examples where there is a very real problem that needs to be solved. Whether we diagnose the problem as being natural versus supernatural has a very real impact on whether the solution is going to be successful and ethical. Choosing reality over supernaturalism is not just a matter of more effective problem-solving. It is usually also an ethical matter because the human rights abuses that occur when scared people blame their fellow humans for their misfortunes are very real.

Ethics and problem-solving are intertwined. The better you can think about them, the better off you will be and the less harm you will cause.

Resistance to Reality

We humans have a problem when it comes to determining what is real. Our problem is that our brains are very imprecise. We make assumptions, we generalize, our sensory organs and our ability to interpret the data our sensory organs are sending to the brain is limited and flawed. Additionally, what we perceive and how we perceive and interpret it is often defined by our frame of reference and prior experiences. You cannot trust your brain to tell you the truth.

A typical example of how our perception tricks us is to consider your perspective when viewing a time lapsed video of the night sky. It looks like the heavens are circling around us. The reality is that we are the ones who are spinning and the stars in the sky are basically fixed in space relative to us. We are the ones who are spinning! Not the stars. When I first told my son about this, he asked an obvious question. If we are moving so fast, why can't we feel it? It is a great question. Our senses tell us we are not moving. The problem is that our senses, in this case, are wrong. This happens more than we would like to admit.

It does not matter what the subject is, if it contradicts our personal experience, we have a hard time embracing new knowledge. I felt this way the first-time plate tectonics was explained to me. A lot of people still feel this way about evolution. When we are exposed to new knowledge, or knowledge that contradicts our personal experience, we resist it.

There are many reasons why people reject reality and refuse to accept new more accurate information, but it usually boils down to this: they are scared of change and there is something about their current view, however wrong it may be, that they are emotionally invested in.

The only thing worse than being wrong is continuing to be wrong. This is especially true in the world of business. To be a good problem solver you must embrace reality. We almost all fear what a change in perspective about the fundamental nature of our reality entails, but once we embrace new knowledge and we correct our perception and understanding of what is really happening, our experience of life becomes richer and deeper.

For instance, knowing that we are the ones doing the spinning does not make the experience of watching the stars move across the skies any less awe-inspiring. Understanding reality makes the experience of reality that much cooler because now you are in on the secret. You see it with fresh eyes and are amazed all the more.

Cost and Consequences of Rejecting Reality

Usually, at this point, people ask me what is the harm? Many of the things that people believe that are not true are harmless. Right? What is the harm in believing in magical power bracelets that improve your balance? What is the harm in reading your horoscope? They may not work, but they may, so what is the harm?

First, let me refer to a website aptly named What's the Harm? (http://whatstheharm.net/). This website details death, disfigurements, and more that result from people not applying critical thinking skills to what they thought were seemingly harmless pseudo-non-science (pun intended).

There are very real costs to believing things that are not true. These costs can be physical, emotional, or financial, often all three. For instance, every year, in my county, five or six families are bilked out of around 25,000 U.S. dollars from a psychic who cons them into giving their money away. This happens every year. The money that was spent on false hope could have been spent on a more tangible solution to these people's problems. Losing money to a charlatan is one potential cost.

I know what you are thinking. That would never happen to you. You are too smart for that. Don't be too sure. The preceding scenario was fairly harmless because all it involved was money. The harm caused by believing things that are not true can also cause physical damage up to and including death. People die every year because they do not take the time to figure out if what they think is true about their medical condition really is true or not. Every year in my state, we prosecute parents whose children died because they attempted faith healings instead of taking them to a doctor.

This loss of life is not limited to people who go to medical charlatans instead of real doctors. You may be smart enough to avoid psychic surgeons, but Steve Jobs, as smart and as well-educated as he was, attempted to treat his cancer with a diet before going to a real doctor. The time he lost by attempting an alternative therapy ultimately cost him his life.

There is an entire anti-vaccination movement that has caused the deaths of countless children because they were skeptical of the science showing the benefits of vaccines, but not skeptical of the flawed science purporting to show a connection between vaccinations and autism that turns out not to exist at all. The anti-vaccination movement is made up of some very smart people. Anyone can be fooled.

The reason we Humanists keep talking about and encouraging people to be skeptical of even the littlest things that are fairly harmless is because we know that critical thinking is a skill that requires practice. If you are not willing to practice these important thinking skills on things that are not that important, how do you know you are going to be able to use them properly when it really does matter?

Real-Life Benefits

There are issues we all encounter every day of our lives that can benefit from a healthy dose of critical thinking. These range from the mundane, like which shampoo should you buy, to the profound, like which politician should you vote for.

Every day you are called on to make decisions. The better you are at figuring out what is true and what is false and what is only kind of sort of true, and what is sometimes kind of false, the better you are going to be at making decisions that have a profound impact on your life and the lives of others.

Critical thinking is the key to making good ethical decisions in all areas of your life. The more you practice it, the better you are going to be at it, and the more effective and ethical your decision making will be.

Critical Thinking 101

Critical thinking is difficult to learn and to master. Even the best thinkers are prone to making mistakes. This is why the best critical thinkers are intellectually humble. We all make mistakes. To do the best job you can requires you to be open to being proven wrong. If you will not change your mind, how do you know you still have one?

If you are new to the whole intellectual humility thing, keep reminding yourself of your primary goal, and that is to base your decisions, as much as possible, on reality. Real reality, not perceived reality.

The benefits of being reality based will far outweigh any humble pie you might need to eat in the process. Plus, being humble enough to admit you were wrong means you are at least smart enough and courageous enough to fix your mistakes, and knowing that about yourself feels pretty good.

There are four basic skills you will want to learn in order to become good at critical thinking. These are scientific literacy, freethought, skepticism, and logic. These skills combine to create a very powerful approach to thinking that will serve you well the more you use them. No one is perfect at this. However, if you make an effort, you will experience the benefit of putting these skills into practice right away, even if you do so imperfectly.

Scientific Literacy

The first skill you will want to learn is how to be scientifically literate. The methods of science are quite simply the best most effective tool we have for discovering objective, as opposed to subjective, knowledge. Science impacts pretty much every aspect of our lives and businesses from what we eat to how we eat it, and everything from energy and housing to disease management and more. It impacts how we solve our problems or whether or not we can solve our problems. At this point, to be an active and engaged citizen of the world, you need to be scientifically literate.

According to the National Science Education Standards: to be scientifically literate, you need to be able to read and understand articles about science and be able to discuss the validity of the conclusions based on the quality of the science and evidence.

This means you need to know what the scientific method is. How it can be used, how it can be misused, and what the most common mistakes are when pursuing knowledge scientifically. You need to know enough to know what constitutes a good or a bad experimental design, whether datasets are valid or not, and whether or not the conclusion may or may not be valid given all of the aforementioned.

Most of all, you are going to want to know whether any given scientific report has enough evidence to back up the claims being made in it. The best way to learn this information is to start reading and finding out what the scientists think. For every study, read the counter-studies. Science progresses through an adversarial process. If one scientist finds out some information, the rest of them go and try to prove the first scientist wrong. The best scientists love this process because, and this will seem weird, but there really is nothing more exciting than learning you were wrong. Because it is when you find out that you were wrong that you truly learn something new.

Regardless, there is only one way to become scientifically literate, and that is to do your reading and your research. In the meantime, we will move on to discuss the other skills you need to think clearly and critically.

Freethought

Freethought is a very difficult skill to master because it consists of identifying and challenging the assumptions you yourself make. As we are rarely aware we are making an assumption, because that is the nature of assumptions, it is really hard to do freethought well.

The goal of the freethinker is to determine, as much as is possible, what is factual. Freethought is most associated with the challenging of religious dogma, but freethinkers do not single out religion for special treatment. We challenge all assumed knowledge from all sources equally. We are equal opportunity doubters.

The hardest part of freethought is learning to challenge your own thinking. It is fairly easy to challenge the thinking of others. A true free-thinker first focuses on making sure their own thinking is free from error. If you have never done this before, be patient with yourself. The more you practice, the easier it gets.

The way I like to get people started is through an exercise I call, The Rule of Threes. There are several applications to this exercise. For the time being I am going to focus on the most important one, and that is to help you combat the false dichotomy, which is one of the most common thinking mistakes we humans make. We seem to be prewired to take a false dichotomy shortcut in our thinking.

A false dichotomy is when you erroneously assume there are only two options (either A or B). Our thinking is filled with these false dichotomies. For instance, what do you want to do for dinner? Eat in or take out?

We almost always have more than two options. We are not taking the time to think about them because, well, that would take time. If you are interested in thinking critically and improving your problem-solving as a result, you need to learn to take the time to think of those other options. The way you do that is to remind yourself, whenever you catch yourself in a dichotomy, is to think of a third option. For instance, when thinking about dinner, you could eat in, take out, or have something delivered. There you have at least three options.

Once you think of a third option, you can often think of a 4th, 5th, 6th, and so on. Once you get past the false dichotomy, the flood gates of creativity can be unleashed. The positive impact this expansion of possi-ble solutions has on your problems-solving abilities results in improved problem-solving as soon as you start to practice it.

For instance, perhaps you have been struggling with deciding whether to do A or B to solve a problem. A quick alternative is to do both A and B. Maybe there is an option C you have not considered yet. You could also choose to do neither A nor B. I just provided three alternatives to the standard do A or B false dichotomy without even straining myself. If you cannot think of at least three options, you simply are not trying.

This technique will not just help you solve your problems better; it will also help you evaluate the claims being made by others as well. Politicians, for example, love to present their ideas as false dichotomies. Either you do it their way or you do it in such a stupid way only an idiot would go along with it. Either you are with us, or against us, is a false dichotomy.

It is not just politicians you need to be wary of. Product sales are often pitched this way as well. Either you buy their product, or your life will be miserable, and no one will like you. The more quickly you can recognize false dichotomies, your own or those of others, the more quickly you can successfully think your way around them and out of them.

Skepticism

Contrary to popular belief, skepticism is an optimistic activity. It is not about rejecting ideas. The purpose of being skeptical is to figure out what is real and what is not. It is about figuring out what will work and what will not. Being a skeptic means believing you have the intelligence and ability to figure out what is objectively true versus what is only assumed to be true.

Being a skeptic means being open to being shown that something new works, but demanding to see the proof that it actually does. The most important question a skeptic can ask is: How do we know that? Is there any evidence to back up the claim being made, or is it a statement of faith?

This brings us to the issue of what is considered acceptable evidence for a skeptic. Acceptable evidence must be physical, verifiable, and repeatable. In other words, it must be scientifically validated. If someone tells you they have no physical proof that what they are saying is true, they just admitted they have no proof. For instance, if I were to tell you I have a flying pig, you would want to see an actual flying pig. Simply telling you there is such a beast would be unlikely to persuade you.

You probably would not accept a video tape of a flying pig either because videos can be faked. You also would not accept a taxidermy pig that had wings as those can be faked. In order to convince you I had a flying pig, you would want to see an actual flying pig with your very own eyes and you would want to examine the pig to make sure that I was not pulling any tricks on you. The evidence required would be both physical and verifiable. Extraordinary claims require extraordinary evidence.

You should also be skeptical if I am the only person who can make a pig fly. If something is true, it is repeatable and not confined to specific situations that only one person can control. If such beasts as flying pigs exist, other people would be able to find them and repeat the experiments to verify that yes indeed, pigs can fly. In the absence of this sort of physical, verifiable, and repeatable evidence, you should be skeptical. Very skeptical. Why? Because people lie when there is money involved!

One of the main reasons you need to be scientifically literate is because much of the evidence presented in scientific papers is in the form of data and statistics. In order to verify if this *evidence* is valid enough to warrant the claim being made, you need to understand statistics, what constitutes a valid sample size (i.e., was this a single instance or several instances?). Is the variation seen in the data statistically significant or a product of chance?

For instance, most of what is taught as generational differences is not statistically significant. If 16 percent of millennials are narcissistic, but only 14 percent of boomers are narcissists, is there really any difference between the groups? No!!! Yet, this sort of claim is made all the time by people who do diversity training.

I am not going to teach you a course in statistics here. Consider this part of your continuing education needs and go borrow a book on statistics from the library. Just understand that that failure to understand this means making mistakes, and mistakes in how you conduct your business are not just costly, they are often unethical and do real harm.

Logic

The final skill you need to learn in order to think well is logic. It is hugely important and probably the funnest critical thinking skill to master. I am not going to go into a whole lot of detail here. If you have not taken a logic class, get a book and start reading. The main things you need to learn are what constitutes a valid argument and why.

The purpose of logic is to ensure that we do not introduce errors into our thinking. Errors can occur in a few different ways. Our premises might be false, and this can lead to false conclusions, which is why knowing what is true and what is not is so important. We can engage in a logical fallacy that would cause our conclusion to be invalid (in other words, not reliable), even if our premises were true. Or, we might have both untrue premises and fallacies, which happens quite a bit.

The goal is to have a valid conclusion. This does not mean your conclusion is true objectively; it only means that you have a higher probability of it being true.

In order to do logic, you need to study the different mistakes we humans are prone to making in our thinking. There are lists of these things. Type in logical fallacies into a search engine to find one. We have already discussed the false dichotomy, which is very common. There are also ad hominen fallacies, red herrings, reverse dogmatic, argument by chorus (which I like to think of as the 50,000 Elvis fans can't be wrong fallacy), and more.

The way to learn this is to start studying the fallacies one by one and to learn how to identify them using real-life examples. Listening to politicians is a great way to find and learn all about fallacies. The same goes for political pundits. As with anything, the more you practice, the better you will get at recognizing the logical fallacies of others, as well as your own.

Putting It All Together

What I want you to get out of all of this is that you need to approach the acquisition of knowledge with all these skills combined together. It is not enough to be skeptical. You also need to be skeptical of your own skepticism which is why freethought is so important. Being skeptical is not enough. You need to do your research to find out whether a claim being made is backed up by the evidence or not (this requires scientific literacy). Otherwise, you are guilty of knee-jerk skepticism, which is not backed up by facts. You need to be able to identify logical fallacies that cause people to make erroneous conclusions based on what is otherwise valid evidence.

For instance, let us consider the anti-vaccination movement as a product of skepticism that did not integrate the other elements of the critical thinking toolkit. The questions they were asking were good, they just did not understand the science enough to know whether what they were being skeptical about was valid or not. They did not take full advantage of their logic skills to be able to detect the fallacies that were and are driving that movement.

It is not enough be skeptical. You must also know how to verify or understand the science you are being skeptical about. Critical thinking skills are interrelated, and you need all of them to think well.

A Framework for Making Good Decision

Now that we know more about what goes into thinking well, let's talk about how a Humanist combines our ethics and our thinking into a powerfully pragmatic problem-solving system. In my opinion, this is the most powerful aspect of the Humanist approach to living. It is the reason most Humanists choose to be a Humanist. Humanism works.

What Is the Problem?

The first thing you want to do is to properly identify your problem. Failure to properly identify your problem will result in you wasting time, money, and energy solving a problem you do not have while the problem you do have continues to plague you. Not a happy prospect for any business person.

A Humanist uses our various critical thinking skills to drill down to the essence of our problem. We use science to determine, if possible, what is actually causing our problem. We use freethought to challenge our assumptions so that we do not assume our problem is caused by A, when it might really be caused by B. We use skepticism to question how we know what we know and whether it is even so and we use logic to make sure we are not making any mistakes before we feel we can safely identify our real problem.

The example I usually give on this in my talks is: when you have a field that needs water. Is your problem that a neighboring tribe put a curse on you, or is it not raining because of weather patterns beyond your control? I like to use this example because it contains an assumption.

That assumption is that our problem is that we need it to rain and it is not raining. That is not really our problem though. It is only what we assume our problem to be. It is a proxy problem.

To get around this assumption, I use freethought and ask myself a series of questions that challenge my thinking until I get to the base problem or my real problem. I call this going Socratic on myself. The question I ask myself is why? Why do I want it to rain? Because I need water on my fields or my plants will die. When I can no longer ask any why questions, I have usually gotten to the real heart of the matter and can start working on solutions.

Making the mistake of solving the wrong problem is very common in business. Whether you are trying to figure out why people are not renewing your service contracts, or you are trying to figure out how to organize your marketing efforts. Taking the time to ask yourself why you are worried about solving any given problem will help you drill down past your assumptions to the heart of the matter that you should really be working on instead.

What Is Actually Causing Your Problem

Once you have properly identified your real problem, you now need to find out what is really causing this problem, and more importantly, whether there is anything you can do about it. What you ideally want to know is whether your problem is caused by something you can change or whether it is something you cannot change.

This is where skepticism and scientific literacy will help you the most. Let me give you a tangible example of this. It was not very long ago that people thought things like epileptic seizures were caused by demonic possession. Their solution to this problem was to perform an exorcism, which was not very effective, and it turns out that people can die during exorcisms. With the introduction of science and skepticism, research was conducted into the possible natural causes of the problem, and it turns out that epilepsy does, in fact, have a natural cause and that it is treatable.

Whatever your problem is, whether you are wondering about how human nature impacts purchases or what chemical might help you best clean work surfaces in your cleaning business; using science to help you understand the root causes of your problem is going to help you come up with a solution that has a better chance of working than basing your solutions on unproven assumptions.

An Ideal Solution

Once you have identified your real problem and done some research to figure out what is actually causing it, it is time to consider what an ideal solution to the problem might be. Here is where a Humanist considers the ethical implications of their actions.

Your ideal solution should integrate your long-term ethics and be geared to solving the problem for yourself and making the world a better place at the same time. For instance, if you are dealing with an energy problem, your ideal solution might be to fix your problem in such a way that you do not create any more pollution than absolutely necessary in the production of that energy while still meeting the price point you need to be competitive, and ideally, having it be a renewable clean energy as well.

The fact that you might not be able to achieve your ideal solution is not really relevant at this stage. The purpose of considering what an ideal solution might look like is because, if you do not have some idea of what an ideal solution might be, you do not have any real way of judging which of your proposed solutions would be the best for you. Stating what your ideal is gives you something to look for and to strive toward. This is the hallmark of humanistic business management. We are not just looking for a solution that will work. We want a solution that will work and accomplish whatever other ethical objectives we might have.

If we were to consider the problem of how best to water our fields, our ideal solution might be to irrigate our fields using a renewable clean source of water that does not run off or cause additional pollution in our water ways, and that does not require a lot of chemical treatment to be used in our fields. We might also want to find a source of water that does not deplete the aquifers and that helps us remain economically competitive all at the same time.

The more specific and holistic you can be about the elements of an ideal solution, the better you are going to be able to assess your possible solutions to find the ones that do good and do not do evil accidentally.

To do this well, do some research to find out what other people are doing and what the pros and cons of the various solutions to your problem currently are. That way, when you design your ideal, you are taking into account known ancillary problems so that your solution can build in fixes to whatever ancillary problems your solution may inadvertently cause.

What Will Actually Work?

Once you have some idea of what your ideal solution might look like, it is time to start researching your options. What you are looking for is a solution that will not only have a high probability of success, but that will help you achieve as much of your ideal as possible.

In my example of your field lacking water, we have already decided we need to get water on the field. One way to do that is for it to rain, the problem is that rain is caused by weather patterns beyond our control. It is renewable and free and basically clean, so it fits those criteria, but it is not reliable. What are our other options?

There are ways to harvest rain water and to store it for future use. There are various ways to irrigate fields using either surface water or aquifers. Each of these potential solutions has pros and cons that need to be addressed and weighed against the ideal. You would be wise to invoke your rule of threes and consider at least three or more potential solutions. What you do not want to do is to only look at the pluses of your potential solutions and ignore their downside.

All our actions have consequences; it is our responsibility to make sure the impact we have is on the balance good and not bad. To do that, we have to do our best to not create new problems for ourselves and for the planet we live on. It is unethical to not consider the potential harm your proposed solutions will cause. You have a moral responsibility to take them into account.

This is where many people fail as managers. They do not want to take on the additional responsibility this approach requires. What they do not realize is that, by taking on this responsibility, you open yourself up to potential solutions that will not just solve your problem; they can revolutionize your business at the same time.

Taking responsibility to solve your problem in a way that does not cause more problems is empowering and liberating. It is the reason why people who do feel morally responsible are so energized about their work and their business and their approach and why their fans and customers are so loyal to them. Ethical problem-solving is inspiring and motivating. It means the work you are doing and the problems you are solving matter. To real people.

Creativity is required to solve your problems in an ideal way. What other possibilities are there? The biggest advances in science and technology come when someone borrows technology and knowledge from one area and applies it to their unrelated problem in a novel way. By refusing to accept solutions that are less than ideal, you open yourself up to finding solutions that are better for everyone. It is this process of continually searching for a better solution that revolutionizes society and the world!

Choosing the Best Option

When you are solving problems as a Humanist, your goal is to get as close to your ideal solution as possible and to continue working on fixes to your problem until you finally achieve that ideal.

Realistically, you cannot always wait until you have an ideal solution. Often, you must take the best solution available to you at the time. This does not mean choosing the first option and hoping for the best. It means evaluating all your various options to see which ones:

- Have a high likelihood of success based on past verifiable experiments and observation
- Are economically feasible
- Do the most good and the least harm in the process of solving your problems
- Have the least downside or whose downside you feel confident you can manage properly, and
- Are closest to your ideal solution

Notice that my first criterion is that it will have a high likelihood of solving your problem in an economically feasible way. If you do not have that, you need to keep looking.

The main thing to realize is that, until you have an ideal solution, your job is not done. Fixing a problem in a less than ideal way means you put a stop gap measure in place to buy yourself some time to continue trying to solve your problem in an ideal way. Do not forget to keep looking for that ideal solution. The truly great business pioneers are those who did not stop working and thinking about ways that they could improve what they were doing to reach their ideals.

CHAPTER 4

Rule #3: R*E*S*P*E*C*T

The people who are the most successful in life are those people who are the best at solving their problems. The people who flourish are those who are able to manage their relationships and their competing responsibilities well. In order to be successful and flourish, you need the help of other people. While there is a lot we can do for ourselves, most problems require the help of others. Plus, among those other people are your customers. Without customers, you have no business.

This is why it is essential to treat everyone you meet with dignity and worth. This is not about liking the person. It is about recognizing that they are indeed a real live human who has their own mind and their own issues and their own problems that likely have nothing to do with you, and if you want to interact with them successfully, you would be wise to recognize that fact.

Purpose

The phrase every human is endowed with dignity and worth means something. This is not just fluffy language meant to encourage us to be nice to each other. When you take the time to think about what it really means, it will change your perspective forever.

Recognizing that each of the seven billion plus people who inhabit planet earth are real live human beings with real minds, real issues, real concerns, real loves, and real hassles that you know nothing about is truly mind blowing.

Humanistic business management is called humanistic business management because it focuses on the reality of the humans you are interacting with on a daily basis, whether they are your staff, your customers, or the people in the community in which your business operates. It is easy to forget that other people are really real, which is why we all need to be reminded of that fact from time to time.

We are all, to a certain extent, trapped in our own heads. We cannot help it. That is where we do all our thinking. The eyes we see out of and the feelings that we feel in our bodies are ours and ours alone. Other people do not experience what we experience. We can theorize that they experience something similar to what we do, but they are not us and their experiences are *their* own. This ability to extrapolate our thinking existence to other people is called the *theory of mind*. It helps us interact with people as if they are humans and alive and not as a rock blocking our path.

As useful as it is to assume that other people think and feel just like you do, your perspective is just that. A perspective. Yes, other people do seem to think and act like you do, but, they are not actually you. They are them. They have their own eyes and their own body and their own feelings and experiences that make up who they are, and that color their understanding of what is happening to *them* at any given moment.

Why Does This Matter?

This matters because reality matters. If you want to interact with people successfully, and I assume you do because your business and your inter-personal relationships depend on you doing this well; you need to under-stand the limitations of applying your perspective to other people. Yes, they have feelings and emotions and are for the most part rational actors. But, their experiences and emotions are not the same as yours. They have their own perspective they are viewing things from. Most importantly, you need to understand that they are not always rational actors. In case you were wondering, you are not always rational either.

Compassion

This is why, I keep talking about the importance of compassion. People are not perfect. They are not going to always behave the way they ide-ally should. You do not either. When that happens, be compassionate with other people in the same way you want them to be compassionate with you.

This does not mean that bad behavior is OK. It means how you deal with it is going to be driven from your compassion, rather than from your anger or frustration. Many of our interpersonal conflicts arise when we try to control other people. Instead of accepting them for who they are and for the limitations they have, we expect them to be perfect and get mad when they are not.

Getting mad does not help anyone, and it does not help you fix the problems that arise as a result of our collective human fallibility. Instead of expecting perfection, build into your operating systems ways to double-check common human mistakes.

For Instance

For instance, if there are conflicts between departments, instead of assuming the other department head has it in for you, why not find out if they have a legitimate reason why they are not getting that thing you need them to do done. It may turn out that you are not providing them with the information they need to do their job. This happens more often than we realize.

If someone wrongs you, do not wait for them to make the first apologetic move. Take responsibility for your side of the conflict by figuring out what you did wrong and what you might have done differently to have avoided the conflict in the first place.

If you think you are wonderful and not at fault, so you should not have to change what you are doing to accommodate someone else, then you are mistaken and a narcissist. We are all flawed. You are flawed. I am flawed. The person you are dealing with is flawed.

In order to get other people to work with and for us optimally, we need to adapt to the needs of the other people we are working with. A humanistic manager has no ego in this regard. The end goal is solving the problem. If they have to swallow their pride to allow another person to *win* in order to accomplish getting the work done, that is what they do. Why? Because you are not in business to feed your ego. Your real goal is effective problem-solving. Never let your ego get in the way of solving a problem.

The World Does Not Revolve Around You

The mistake we make when we are in our own heads reacting to things from our perspective is that we tend to think that our perspective is the correct one. The problem is, so does the other person. To get them to help you solve your problem, you need to make an effort to understand their perspective. To do that, you first must have compassion with yourself and accept the fact the other person is another flawed human just like you. They are responding to their own issues and concerns and experiences.

Once you understand that, for them, it is all about what they are experiencing; you can adjust your behavior to help them see the benefit of helping you. Yes, this really does work. No, it is not dishonest. It is a compassionate, rational, dignified, and effective way to deal with all your interpersonal relationships and the people you interact with will love you if you can master this.

Let us take a look at a few examples of how dignity, respect, and compassion combine to help you in different aspects of your business.

Customers

The first most obvious area where being respectful and compassionate will help you is with your customers. Your customers are real human beings, and the reason they buy your products and services has to do with their needs, their wants, their dreams, their desires, and their problems. They probably do not care much about the fact that, if you do not make a sale, your family will go hungry. That is not their concern. Their concern is their family and their needs.

The way to get someone's business is to help them fix their problems, and you cannot do that if you do not actually care about them or their problems. There is an added consideration, and that is that all things being equal; most people would rather do business with a person they actually like than with someone they do not.

Being compassionate gives you a competitive edge because it helps you connect in a real way with your customers. It also helps you enjoy your work more because wouldn't you rather be working with people you like and enjoy? Yes, of course you would. The way to transform customers into people you like and enjoy is to extend your compassion to them.

Harnessing Compassion

When you treat your customers as the individuals they are, you understand that, while they might have a lot in common with your other customers, their situation is unique to them. Yes, their particular problem may be quite common, but that does not mean it is common to them.

The absolute masters of this sort of compassionate individualized customer care are funeral directors. They deal with people who are grieving all day every day as part of their job. To a certain extent, there is a formula they use to help families not only grieve, but deal with the legalities of a funeral and the actual details of the funeral itself. Within that framework, everything is customizable to the needs of the grieving family. Their customers come from every background, every belief and non-belief, and every economic group. They are flexible, respectful, and compassionate enough to do justice to each unique individual they are helping to bury or cremate and their families.

Interestingly enough, it is precisely because they have a formulaic framework they work from that allows them to customize their services. The framework they have is designed to provide structure for the general services they provide, yet flexible enough to allow for customization for the customers. I do hope you noticed that customize and customer share the same root word.

It is when we take a compassionate and dignified approach in our businesses, treating our customers with the same sort of compassionate care a funeral director does, we start to see the benefits of this approach. When we build our sales process with customization in mind, we can provide for the unique needs of our customers while also streamlining our efforts.

We can and should be using our businesses to help improve the well-being of our customers, and by doing so, help our brand and our business.

For Example

When I was working in mergers and acquisitions, we used this knowledge to our advantage. We knew that most acquisitions followed a certain path, so we designed our closing processes to handle the most common problems in a routine way. Everyone knew what was supposed to happen and why. We hired people whose sole job was to hold the hands of our sellers and walk them through this process to keep them informed of what was happening and where things were in the process. This was the human touch. It helped us close our deals because it helped make sure our sellers did not get cold feet or feel like we were not paying attention to them in those parts of the process where all you can do is wait for a survey to be completed or when an inevitable problem popped up. Whatever the issue was, their hand-holder was always there to help take care of the emotional needs of their sellers and see to their well-being.

The reason this system worked so well was that we figured out a way to personalize our attention to our sellers to help them cope with what was for them a rather emotional experience, but that was for us rather routine. We were closing about eight deals a week on average. That is a *lot* of acquisitions and a lot of sellers. Despite doing that many deals, we treated each seller as the special and unique individuals they were by planning for that personalized aspect of our deals and building it into our processes.

What really made this system work was that we also planned for the exceptions. When a deal had a problem outside of the norm that made closing it difficult or impossible, we had an exception processing system ready to handle and take over those deals that could not be closed through the routine system. This helped make sure our routine system continued to hum along at a nice clip without getting bogged down with a deal that was problematic. This exception process helped us make sure those difficult deals did not get lost either.

This is very similar to the way tech companies handle their customer service. They hire staff to handle the most routine and regular problems that occur. They also have the folks *downstairs* who handle the truly difficult problems that the routine staff is not equipped to deal with.

The companies that do this well make sure every customer feels unique, and they are able to pass on the issues they cannot handle up the line seamlessly. The ones that do it the best empower the intake staff to manage the problem until it is resolved to the satisfaction of the customer. There are very large companies that do indeed take this approach and their customers are extremely loyal to them as a result.

Those companies who view customer services after a sale as an annoyance are those companies that end up having horrid reputations and who lose out on repeat customers. Why? Because who would you rather deal with? A company that actually cares enough about you as a customer to take care of you properly and whose staff are empowered to help you? Or a company that cannot be bothered?

The Real Reason to Take This Seriously

The real reason to make it a priority to treat each and every one of your customers as the dignified individual they are is because it makes for happier staff. It is demoralizing to have someone call up with a problem and not be allowed to help them because the company you work for will not let you.

Having unhappy staff and unhappy customers is not good business and not good for your business. When employees are empowered to fix customer problems and are encouraged to be truly compassionate with the people they are tasked with helping, you are encouraging them to make real human connections. The benefits of finding real human connections with your customers are immense. It makes working more pleasant because, for the most part, people respond to good vibes with reciprocated good vibes, and that makes for a much more pleasant work environment for your staff and your customers. Empowering your staff to truly look after the well-being of your customers creates space for them to flourish as individuals. It is just good business to approach customers this way.

As for those customers who are cranky and mean, well, it turns out compassion helps to defuse some of that negativity too. Your staff will be better able to deal with the angry and mean customer if they approach them with compassion instead of reciprocating their frustration and anger. This approach will also help make sure that your other customers are not negatively affected by an angry customer.

For Example

I once was at a rental car place returning a car and one of the other customers was rude and mean to the staff, complaining loudly for everyone to hear about how unfair and unreasonable the staff were being with him. The staff did not yell back, they simply kept working on solving this man's problem as compassionately as they could. It turned out that this man was upset for reasons that had nothing to do with his transaction with the rental car company. His real problem was that his regular car was in the shop for over a month, and there was a further delay in repairing it, and, so he had to extend the rental agreement, and he was upset about that and he did not want to do the paperwork required to extend the rental, and that was what he was complaining about. The staff did not allow his anger to upset them. They simply treated him with compassion and got the paperwork done as quickly and as efficiently as they could. Even though this man did not reciprocate the kindness he was being shown, the rest of us there could see that they really were doing right by him and helping him as best they could under the circumstances. They earned a customer for life in me that day because I now know they will treat me with the same care if I am ever in a bind or panicked about my car situation.

The benefits of helping your staff learn how to treat even the most difficult customer with compassion is staff that does not get burnt out from dealing with cranky customers all day even if that is what they are doing.

Compassion helps your staff deal with the various personalities that are your customers with an emotional equilibrium that you cannot get if you are thinking selfish and hurtful thoughts. The reason funeral directors are, for the most part, happy people, despite dealing with death and grief all day is because they know they are truly helping people who are not in a position to reciprocate the love and care that they are being given. That is OK. Giving compassion really does feel so good that you do not need it reciprocated.

Employees

The second area where you should exercise compassion is with your employees. Humanistic managers care about the well-being of their employees. Employees who feel valued are more likely to be loyal to and stick with a company, so you will have less turnover. Employees who feel valued are also happy employees and happy employees make for a much happier workplace and happier customers.

As with all people, your employees are unique individuals. Most want to do well and want to like the people they work with and for. As with customers, you need to design your work processes with the majority in mind and have processes in place to deal with the exceptions. Because, while most people are basically good people who want to do well at their job, there are occasionally people who are not.

I want to caution you, before you write someone off as a bad apple. First, consider whether you failed to provide them what they needed as a manager, or whether the role you had assigned them was not a good fit for their personality. I once worked in a department where our team was made up almost entirely of people who had been fired from other departments. We were a band of misfits and castoffs. We were also one of the most productive groups in the company. The reason for that was our manager was *very* savvy and compassionate, and he understood that different people need different work environments, and that a good manager provides that for them.

Some people need more direction and enjoy having regular oversight of their work to ensure that they are not making mistakes. Some need more autonomy and the authority to make decisions in their area of expertise. It is an amazing thing to see someone who has been rejected from one team turn into a brilliant and respected member of another team.

In my experience, most employee problems are a result of problems with management, and not a problem with the ability, skills, or interest of the employee. Treating employees with dignity and compassion makes all the difference in the world, and when done well, allows employees to truly flourish within the organization.

How Does This Work?

In order to help place the right person in the right role and to provide them with the right work environment so that they can thrive, you need to recognize that your employees are not robots, nor are they cogs in a machine. They are real live human beings with a spectrum of abilities, proclivities, and temperaments. You are not just looking for people willing to work who have the skills you want, you also need to make sure that you have properly assessed what the different jobs need so that you can fit the right personality into the right job.

For instance, perfectionists might not make great hand-holders, but they make great due diligence and Q&A folks. Social butterflies might have all the skills needed to do your cad drawings, but they might actually be happier and more effective in a role that allows them to be the conduit of information between teams. Here are seven steps to keep in mind when hiring, training, and managing staff in a humanistic management framework.

Step 1: Recognize the individual for who they are as a whole person, and not just as someone with specific knowledge you think might be helpful.

Step 2: Provide them with the right work environment so that their personality and skills can be utilized fully and not suppressed because you as the manager cannot figure out how to take advantage of their unique abilities and temperament.

Step 3: Ensure that your staff are properly oriented. They need to understand the big picture, how their part of the work fits into the rest of the organization, and how the different pieces inter-relate to create the whole. A good orientation explains how everyone in the company is dependent on everyone else doing their job in order for the company to work effectively. Make sure they know how important their work is, even if what you are asking them to do is sweep your floors. It is all essential or you would not have hired them.

Step 4: Make sure they have the training they need to do the job. If you hire someone to sweep your floors, but you do not ensure they know how to use a broom, they probably are not going to succeed.

Step 5: Verify that they have learned your specific and unique processes. Do not assume it is obvious. Every work group has its quirks. Even sweeping the floor for a company has quirky requirements. Do not omit those during training or you set your employee up for failure. If they do fail, do not treat them as a failure; it was your fault as the manager that you did not teach them this quirk.

If they come up with a solution to a problem and it is not the solution you hoped for, understand that they are creatively solving a problem, and that is a good thing. Do not punish them for that. Learn why what you thought was going to work—did not and how the processes need to be adjusted to take into account—the reality the employees experience.

Step 6: In the early stages of an employee's work for you, check their work and help them learn from the mistakes made in Step 4. It is amazingly disheartening to think you are doing something correctly and doing it for a long time only to find out that you have been doing it wrong all along and no one bothered to tell you. No one feels good about that. When this happens, it is the manager's fault. The sooner you can help an employee identify a problem and correct it, the happier everyone will be. The longer you let something linger, the more frustration and anger will arise when you finally do correct it.

Step 7: Thank them for their work. Do not take it for granted that they were going to do it anyway. People like to know you appreciate their work. The key to doing this step well is to understand that different individuals need different rewards for their work. In order to provide them with a reward that is meaningful to them, you need to know what is motivating them. It is not just that people are getting paid for their work. That is nice, but it is not all people want.

I started my professional career working in volunteer management. With volunteers, you do not reward them with pay. You have to provide them with another reason to volunteer for you. Some people want public recognition. Some people are looking for friendships, some are looking to learn new skills, and some get really excited when they accomplish something difficult that they did not think was possible. In order to keep your employees happy and loyal, you need to treat them as the individuals they are and figure out what is motivating them so that you can individualize your approach for each employee. This sounds harder than it actually is. Break down the most common motivations and design your rewards and thank-you programs to provide the customized motivation your different employees require. Structured flexibility really does work.

Most managers fail at this because they are only really comfortable working with people who are basically like them and motivated by the same things as they are. A humanistic business manager stretches themselves out of their comfort zone to make sure they are treating each of their employees with dignity and celebrate the unique gifts and traits that each brings to the company. After all, if you have a company of like-minded individuals, you are limiting yourself and your problem-solving and your customer base to people who are like you. That is not good for business.

Truly Bad Apples

The fact that most employee management problems are the fault of the manager does not mean they all are. Every once in a while, you will come across an employee who lies, cheats, or steals. You also come across the occasional aggressive individual who bullies and intimidates anyone who disagrees with them. Part of the job of the manager is to protect the other employees and the company from this sort of abuse.

The challenge is how to identify these individuals quickly so that the negative impact they have on your team and your business is minimized. Bullies and other unethical individuals are usually really good at lying and getting away with it. The bullying factor also plays into this. Unethical people are very good at intimidating others into not reporting their bad behavior or of giving the impression that what they are doing is actually OK and condoned by the managers and leadership of the company.

Most of your staff have been conditioned from childhood that there is really no point in reporting the bad behavior of others because nothing good ever comes from such reporting. All that happens is that you draw the anger of the bully onto yourself. As a result, when a bad apple enters your workspace, most of your employees are going to keep their heads down and their mouths shut and secretly hope that a miracle will occur and that this bad apple will go away on his or her own so that they do not have to give up a job they actually like.

As much as you would like your employees to tell you: hey, you know that guy Joe, he is not doing his job or he is stealing from the cash register or he is sexually harassing the customers, they are not likely to tell you that. It is not enough to put in place a no tolerance policy. It is not enough to have a whistleblower program. You need to cultivate a culture of ethics that permeates the entire company. Model the ethical behavior you expect from your employees. Actively be honest and ethical and compassionate in order to give courage to the good people who work for you to not tolerate the truly bad ones. Make conversations about ethics a regular part of the problem-solving process so that your staff knows you are not just talking about ethics, you expect them to be put into daily practice.

You also need to find a way to empower your employees to report things to you that they do not feel comfortable about so that they do come to you when they feel ethically uncomfortable. They need to know that their concerns will be handled discreetly, and that you will be fair and impartial when looking into any allegation of misconduct. Mostly, what they want and need to see from you as their manager is that you take their concerns seriously and will act upon it accordingly. You, as the manager, need to hold the hands of the person who did the reporting and positively reward them so that they know that what they did was worthwhile. Obviously, while an investigation is ongoing, there are privacy issues to take into consideration. You can still let the reporting employee know that it is being looked into discretely and possibly where it is in the process even if you do not give them any details of what you have learned so that they do not start thinking nothing came of reporting, so there is no point in reporting in the future.

All of this advice is actually science-based. How people respond to rewards and consequences is well studied, and we can use that to create processes that reward the behavior we want (reporting of unethical behavior) and discourage the behavior we do not want (unethical behavior).

Work–Life Balance

The final area you need to have compassion for is the area of work–life balance. I have a friend, who for the first time in about five years, is working for a company that respects the need for work–life balance. It has taken him a while to get used to the fact that he really is done with his work at 6 pm and does not have to bring it home with him. He is now in a position to finally get a life.

One of the main goals of a Humanist is to live a happy and productive life. We like work. It provides a focus and a reason to get up in the morning. But, there is more to life than work. In order to have a full and fulfilling life, we need to have balance between our personal, professional, and private lives. It is impossible to flourish as an individual without this balance.

A humanistic manager understands this and seeks to find a good balance for themselves and their employees. They make this a priority. Respect yourself enough to give yourself that balance and care enough about your employees' well-being to insist on it for them. There is no need to feel guilty for having a personal and a private life in addition to your professional life. It is what you should be striving for.

Being at the office early and leaving late and taking your work home with you on the weekends and being on call all the time is not healthy. It is not something you should be modeling for your staff. There is a *really* good reason for this. The extra hours worked and the extra time billed do not mean increased productivity. It is a sham. It is not unusual for everyone in an office to engage in a game of one up to show how busy they are and how much work they need to do and how they cannot possibly do what you asked them to do because they are just too busy to do anything. They cannot even return phone calls they are so busy. This situation happens when managers reward people who appear to be busy instead of rewarding people who get their work done in a timely fashion.

When this sort of *too busy to actually be productive* culture sets in, and it most certainly will if work–life balance is not prioritized, you end up with a lot of really stressed out people who are not getting anything done and those who do are seriously unhappy. In addition, you will have a lot of unnecessary over time being billed.

If there is too much work to do and not enough time to get it done, you need to hire more people to get it done. Or, you need to figure out how to be more efficient in your processes so that unnecessary stuff gets cut out of the process. Or, you need to prioritize better. There are at least three ways to fix the *too much work to do* problem. More, if you get creative. The first step is to be honest about how much time tasks really take and to budget your time accordingly.

Whenever I am tasked with something new, my first question is, when do you need this by? If it is an unrealistic timeline, I tell my manager that. I do not do them or anyone else any good if I lie and take on the extra work. What ends up happening is that I get stressed out, the work does not get completed or does not get completed well, and that becomes the norm, rather than the exception.

In order to prevent that from happening, you need to model pragmatic and realistic time management as the manager. You need to make sure that all conversations involving projects that need to be done include a candid discussion of time requirements so that you can allocate the right resources to get the job done effectively, and you need to empower your employees to be realistic themselves about what it really takes to get a job done and reward them when they are honest and tell you—it cannot be done with the time and resources that were allocated.

Everyone wants to go home at a reasonable time and your staff does too. Chalk this up to pragmatic problem-solving. If you cannot be realistic about time management because everyone is too scared to admit that what is being asked is unrealistic and they do not want to appear as if they are not committed to getting the job done, then you are not going to get honest answers and feedback on solving your other problems either.

Respect yourself and your employees enough to make the late nights and weekend work incredibly rare, as opposed to normal. Everyone will be happier, and your productivity and employee retention will go up dramatically.

Always remember, the idea that you either work late or this project does not get done is a false dichotomy. Think of at least three other ways you might be able to solve this dilemma that will help you get home on time and get the project done. A Humanist manager simply does not accept the status quo if the status quo is going to make people suffer.

Humanizing Your Business

The biggest aspect of humanistic business management is that, by adopting this strategy, you are actively and intentionally humanizing your business. It is very easy to get caught up in the day-to-day tasks and your own stresses and your own to-do list and to forget that the reason you have a business in the first place is to help other people. All businesses are in the problem-solving business. Inanimate objects do not have problems that need to be solved. Humans do.

By remembering that you are working to help humans, that you work with and for humans, and that the entire enterprise of business is being conducting by and for humans, changes how you think about your job and conduct your business.

This is not just about making money, though that is nice. What gives your business meaning and purpose is the fact that humans are involved in it and hopefully being positively impacted by your business. Let this sink in for a bit before reading further.

I do not know about you, but I find the idea of humanizing my business inspiring. Keeping the human element in mind transforms a job from a job to a calling. It is much easier to be inspired to go to work in the morning if you know you are helping other people as a result of your work.

We humans need this. It is our relationships with other people that give our lives meaning. It helps us feel connected and less alone in the universe to know that we are actively engaged with other humans in this collective endeavor we call life.

The reason why business people are turning to humanistic business management as an approach to their jobs is because it is not only yields better results; it is also emotionally satisfying. Taking a humanistic approach to business is good for business; it leads to increased feelings of well-being and helps promote human flourishing.

CHAPTER 5

Rule #4 It Is Your Responsibility

One of the strengths of Humanism is that it is a philosophy grounded in the idea of human agency. This basically means that we think that we can, by choosing our actions wisely, positively affect our world. Because we believe we have the ability to impact the world, we also believe we have a moral responsibility to make sure our impact is good.

Humanism affirms our ability and responsibility to lead ethical lives of personal fulfillment that aspire to the greater good of humanity. When you take the time to consider what it means to accept the responsibility for shaping not only the course of your life, but the impact you will have on others, it changes everything.

A lot of people treat the word responsibility as if it is a bad thing. The flawed thinking is that, in order to be happy, we need to be free, and responsibility hinders our freedom. In a business world, this is often formulated as we need to be free to conduct our business however we want, or we will not be successful. We Humanists do not buy into that nonsense. This sort of immature reasoning is usually only invoked by people who are doing bad things and do not want to be held responsible for the harm they are causing.

A Humanist, instead of rejecting responsibility, embraces it and all that it entails. A Humanist knows that responsibility is the key to attaining freedom and, therefore, happiness. We know that, if we do not accept this responsibility and take it seriously, we will never achieve what we might otherwise have accomplished.

By being responsible for your actions, you gain control over the consequences of your actions. From a Humanist perspective, you can either be a victim of fate or be the designer of your destiny. Which one sounds better to you?

It Is Your Choice

Ultimately, the way you choose to live your life is a choice only you can make. Most people never consciously make that choice; they just float along hoping for the best, and at some point, they end up in a midlife crisis questioning who they are.

The reason Humanists choose to be responsible is because we realize, whether we like it or not, we are the ones who have to live with the consequences of our actions. We can either choose our actions wisely or we can make random choices and hope for the best. We choose to choose wisely.

To help make this choice easier, let me share a little secret with you. The people who are happiest and most effective at life are those who have chosen to be responsible. Here is why.

First, if you want to be more successful in life, make good decisions. Responsible people take decision-making very seriously, and so, tend to make better decisions. As a result, they tend to be more successful in all areas of their lives.

Second, it is really hard to be happy if you are making yourself and others miserable through your actions or rather inactions. By taking responsibility for your actions, you change not only the entire dynamic in which you make your decisions, you also are able to integrate your ethics and values into your decision-making, and this helps you to not only make better decision, it also helps you improve your interpersonal relationships, both in your private and public lives.

Third, most people need to have a sense of meaning and purpose in their lives to feel fulfilled. By taking responsibility for your life and your actions and your consequences, you can choose to integrate your ethics into how you live your life, and this choice helps you have both meaning and purpose in your life.

Finally, when you take responsibility for your choices, you start to live life intentionally. You are not just floating along hoping for the best, you are in command. You are actively choosing how you will act and be. Not only for the big decisions, but with the little ones as well.

Living life intentionally is invigorating. Life coaches talk about this in terms of living at peak performance. I like this analogy. That is basically what it feels like. All the time. It is invigorating and empowering. Humanists do not have a problem with motivation.

The quickest most effective and most ethical way to achieve that peak performance of living life intentionally at all times is to accept responsibility for your choices, all your choices, including those times when you choose not to choose.

Taking responsibility for all our actions is the foundation of our freedom. It not only provides the basis for our personal well-being, but it helps us create the conditions in which we can flourish.

Limitations and Liabilities

The great news about choosing to be responsible is that it is empowering. It feels great to be the captain of your destiny, and not simply wait for fate to play her hand. As much power as you get from choosing to be responsible for your actions, that power is not absolute. The reason it is not absolute has several causes. One is a rather complex metaphysical idea called *swerve*, the other reasons are a bit more mundane.

First, the only person you can control is yourself, and even then, depending on how you are physically feeling and whether you had a proper lunch and enough sleep, you may not be able to control yourself as much as you would like. Regardless, the fact that you can only control yourself means that other people you are dependent on may choose not to cooperate with your vision of the future. Because you cannot force people to cooperate, you need to accept this limitation as reality and plan accordingly.

Second, however much you would like to be a rational actor capable of choosing your responses to the things that are happening around you, you are still an animal with animal instincts that have been fine-tuned and honed throughout the course of your life. This basically means there are aspects of your behavior that are so conditioned, they have become habits, and habits are very hard to break. You are not always as in control as you should be. This is a matter of accepting reality so that you can adjust your expectations and your strategy accordingly to exert more control over your choices and actions even when it is difficult to do so.

Finally, you can only control your life so much. Chance also plays a role. As much as you might want something to happen, you cannot make it happen by wishing for it. There are random things that happen that are outside of anyone's control, and they can have a huge impact on your life.

I am writing this shortly after Hurricane Michael hit the panhandle of Florida. In one day, people's lives were changed. People died, people were born, businesses and homes were destroyed. They had no control over this happening. But, thanks to science, most had the ability to get out of the way and live to see another day.

I am not telling you this to depress you. I simply feel that the more we face reality, the more effective we are going to be at dealing with reality. The good news is that, even though you cannot control everything in your life, you still can control an amazing amount.

If you are to live your life fully and intentionally, it helps to be optimistic, despite it all. However hard it gets, and it can get really hard, a Humanist will get through it by thinking, well what am I going to do about this? Die? Give up? If the answer is no, you plan to keep on living, then you have basically chosen to continue living, despite it all, and having made that choice, you might as well make the best of it and do your best. It makes no sense to choose to continue living and not actively work to make your life and the lives of others better.

So yes, a Humanist is optimistic. But, we are not blindly so. Our vision of a better future for ourselves and for others is what drives us to get up every day and do whatever it is that we do. How we go about making our vision a reality is very pragmatic, down to earth and realistic.

For people who are into the power of positive thinking, the Humanist approach can seem rather negative. Nothing could be further from the truth. A Humanist simply recognizes the limitations of positive thinking and takes active steps to compensate for those limitations so that we will have a higher likelihood of success.

For instance, when doing strategic planning, a Humanist will spend time thinking of all the ways things can go wrong. We are not drawing negative energy to us. That is a magical idea. What we Humanists are really doing is grounding ourselves in a pragmatic approach. We are identifying potential problems so that we can plan to avoid those pitfalls from the start. We do not like having our progress derailed because we did not plan properly.

We view this sort of reality-based problem-solving to be a very optimistic thing to do. It is based on the belief that we can not only solve our problems, we can be proactive in preventing problems from occurring in the first place. By taking a pragmatic and proactive approach, as opposed to magical thinking and hoping approach, we can not only limit our liabilities, we can compensate for our limitations as well, giving ourselves a greater chance of success.

Playing the Odds

Given the challenges and given the fact that there are no guarantees even if you do choose to take charge of your life by choosing to be responsible for your choices and your actions, how exactly does this help you improve your life?

The answer is that choosing your actions wisely, even though it does not guarantee success, it does change the odds for success in your favor. If you are able to change the odds in your favor on a daily basis, over time, those odds add up to more success and less hardship. There are no guarantees you will succeed. What you get is an improvement of your chances for success. This might not seem like a lot, but it actually provides tremendous help to people who choose to take advantage of this aspect of reality.

Here Is How This Works

To better understand this concept, let us consider the odds of getting into a bad car accident. If you choose to drive drunk, are you guaranteed to get into a car accident? No. Of course not. All you are doing is increasing the odds that you will get into a car accident. If you drive sober, is that a guarantee that you will not get into a car accident? No. All driving sober does is decrease the odds of you getting into a car accident.

Your choices, *all* of your choices, change the odds of certain things happening. Some of these potential consequences are good, some are bad. If you make good decisions, you increase the odds of good things happening to you. If you make bad decisions, you increase the odds of bad things happening to you. This is a very easy concept to understand, and it underlines how important it is to make good decisions if you want to be successful.

There are no guarantees. However, given how easy this is to do and given how much benefit it provides, there is no reason why you should not take advantage of any opportunity to improve your odds. The key is to consciously choose to be responsible for making good decisions that will benefit you and everyone else.

This last part is really the key to a Humanist conception of success. Many people use this knowledge to tilt the odds in their favor at the expense of others. You can use this power for good, or you can use it to gain an unfair advantage. A Humanist chooses to use this power to benefit themselves and everyone else because they understand that any short-term gains they may get from hurting others or hurting the environment is increasing the odds that they are going to have to deal with the very real consequences of causing harm to others.

Additionally, knowingly causing harm to other people represents a failure of ethics, and it means you are not a good person. People who are seeking a good balance between professional and personal success will not sacrifice their personal success in this way. Period.

A Humanist will always weigh the potential benefit and harm to themselves against the potential benefit or harm they may cause to others before making a decision. A Humanist tries their best to make decisions that benefit everyone, including themselves. That is why they are considered Humanists.

The benefit of choosing to be altruistic in decision-making is enormous. First, people who do this tend to be more successful at achieving their aims without sacrificing their morals in the process. Though they choose this path in order to have a clear conscious for themselves, they also gain the respect of their communities for considering the humanistic impact they are having on others in everything they do. This, in turn, helps them draw good people to them, which makes their lives and their work easier as they have good people supporting them.

Their interpersonal relationships, both privately and professionally, tend to be stronger too because people can trust them because they are truly worthy of that trust because they take the needs of others into consideration and do not act out in a selfish manner.

While it is possible to gain some success by cheating and hurting people, it is very hard to truly flourish if you are not concerned about the well-being of others.

Maybe you can get away with cheating on your spouse or dumping chemicals into a nearby stream, but at what cost? Are you really willing to pay that cost, should you get caught? That is what being responsible is about. You choose your actions, and so choose your consequences. If you choose to behave in a way that harms yourself or other people, you are responsible for bringing those negative consequences on yourself and others. If you choose actions that harm other people, at some point, you have to expect them to fight back against you. Why bring that on yourself?

For me, the main value of this Humanist approach is that, by choosing your actions wisely to benefit both yourself and others, you do not attract extra trouble. Life is hard enough as it is. There are enough challenges to overcome in your quest to be successful. I find it incredibly idiotic to add more burdens and worries to your path by being unethical or by choosing actions that you know will increase the odds of bad things happening to you. Do not do that to yourself. Choose to be responsible and choose to be the best most ethical person you can be. You will be amazed at how much easier life is when you do.

Why This Is Better than Wishful Thinking

The other reasons why choosing to be responsible for your actions and for changing the odds in your favor is because wishful thinking is not enough. If you want to be successful, take positive action to achieve that success.

I am an author. In order to be a successful author, I can't only dream about it. I actually have to write a book. No amount of positive thinking is going to help me become a successful author if I do not take that first necessary step and write a book. Having written a book is not enough either, I can change the odds of my book becoming a success by marketing it and publicizing it. This requires me to do something more than just dream and think positive thoughts. It requires me to take action to change the odds in my favor. Even if I do everything right, write a wonderful book, get wonderful reviews, do wonderful marketing, my book still might not be successful. By taking these steps, what I am doing is increasing the odds of my success over people who just dream and hope.

I do not want to downplay the importance of dreaming and hoping. Our dreams give us the motivation to take action. A Humanist takes it further and knows that, in order for something positive to happen, we have to take positive action to help make it happen.

Rising to the Challenge

For many people, being responsible is a scary prospect. A Humanist views it as empowering. Knowing we have the ability to rise to the challenges of life. Knowing that we have the ability to improve our life if we choose to be responsible is what helps us rise to the challenge of taking full responsibility for improving our lives and the lives of others.

While we Humanists choose this approach because of the benefits to ourselves, the real reason we do so is because we feel morally committed to helping others as much as we can. This is not something we give lip service to. It is a commitment and a choice and a responsibility to others that infuses our life with meaning and purpose. Our commitment to doing good for ourselves and for the well-being of others helps us feel connected and alive and vibrant.

What seems to hold people back from making a commitment to be a courageously moral person is fear. They do not know if they are capable of that much responsibility. They do not know if they can handle it emotionally. After all, feeling morally responsible for the impact you have on everyone in the world is a lot of responsibility. It is too much for many people to even contemplate.

Those who do rise to this challenge and commit to being the best, most ethical person they can be in all that they do find that their lives are transformed in such a profound way, they wonder why they ever resisted committing to being the best most ethical person they can be in the first place.

This changes how you view and treat other people. It changes how you go about making decisions. It gives you a framework to think through problems, and it helps you feel courageous and connected and with a purpose that resonates strongly in your heart. All it takes is a choice to face your fears and to embrace reality, as scary as it might seem, and a commitment to be the best you can be despite it all.

Yes, you still have to work hard. You still have to put in an extra effort to improve your thinking and your decision-making skills to make sure you are basing your decisions on reality, and not fantasy. You have to actively practice compassion in difficult situations and with difficult people. But it is worth it, and as you become more practiced at this, it becomes easier.

The biggest benefit is that rising to the challenge of truly embracing your compassionate ethics and embracing reality fully, the good and the bad, is that it will help you solve your problems more effectively and in a way you can be proud of.

This approach makes life easier. There is a reason why every major philosopher and religious leader throughout history taught some form of this approach and emphasized the need to be compassionate and ethical. When you truly commit to solving problems in an ethical, compassionate, and realistic way, you will find that your problem-solving abilities improve dramatically. Problems that used to plague you melt away as you are better able to prioritize your problems and focus your energy on areas that truly matter, and that you can have a positive impact on. Most importantly, the act of choosing to be the best most ethical person you can be transforms your entire outlook on life. It provides a clarity that you didn't even know you were missing and helps you really own the good person you are striving to be. To reap these benefits, choose to rise to the challenge of truly being responsible for your actions.

Balancing Your Responsibilities

Once you have chosen to be responsible for the impact of your actions, not just on yourself but on others, the next question is how? How can you balance your needs against the needs of others and still be ethical, compassionate, responsible, and realistic?

The key is to accept that it is your responsibility to balance your responsibilities to yourself and others, and that this balancing is an active process. You cannot set your life balance levels on autopilot and forget them. Believe it or not, accepting that it is your responsibility to balance your responsibilities is the hardest part. Once you accept that responsibility and take it seriously, you will find choosing how to balance your competing responsibilities becomes easier.

This is just something you have to do. Fussing and whining about how much you do not want to do it is not going to make the problem go away. All that you are doing is choosing not to choose. You still have to deal with the consequences of that choice, and those consequences are usually a lot of stress because you still have not decided how you are going to balance it all.

The only thing that will make the stress go away is making a conscious choice to choose your priorities and then choosing your responsibilities wisely. Rational thinking will help here, and that is why, it is so important.

The key to finding a good balance is to understand that this is an active, rather than a passive activity. What works for you one day may need to be re-evaluated the next. As your situation changes, as your abilities change, as the need arises, you must constantly weigh your responsibilities to yourself, to your family, to your business, to your community, and to the world in which you live. No, this is not always an easy thing to do, but it is your responsibility to figure out how to find balance, so stop procrastinating and just do it.

The way I find balance is by considering my competing responsibilities as a hierarchy. This helps me figure out how to balance my responsibilities in a way that benefits me and everyone else. Here is how I prioritize my responsibilities.

Yourself

My first responsibility is to myself. If I do not take care of myself, I cannot take care of others. This knowledge was earned the hard way through my work at a non-profit. You can only give so much before you will make yourself sick. Take care of yourself so that you can take care of others. You are not being selfish when you do this.

You are only being selfish if you use the need to take care of yourself as an excuse to abandon your responsibilities to others. If you choose to solve your balance problem by abandoning all other responsibilities, you are not finding balance, you are being selfish.

Prioritizing yourself is not the same thing as abandoning your responsibilities to others. Never forget that you matter as much as everyone else does, and you should take yourself and your needs into account when figuring out what the best balance is. Do not feel guilty about putting yourself first. You are not super human, you are human. This means you need to accept your limitations and deal with them realistically.

Your ultimate goal is to figure out what you need to take care of yourself, and if possible, to help others as well. Prioritize your well-being.

Your Family

Your next priority is your family and friends. In order to be happy and healthy, you need good people around you. We humans are social animals. We thrive if we have a tribe and suffer when we do not. Do not neglect your family and friends.

One of the main regrets of people on their death beds is that they did not spend enough time with their family and friends. Do not make this mistake. If you do not prioritize your family and friends, you will not make sure you have enough time to spend with them.

Do not use this as an excuse to not take care of strangers and others in your community. The goal is to find balance. Make sure you include the well-being of your family and friends in that balance and you will do fine.

Your Business

Your next priority is your business or your job. In order to survive and thrive, you need some way to make a living. Make sure you prioritize making a living.

Ideally, you should be looking for work or businesses that can help you achieve your other priorities to your family and to your community and to the world as well. Obviously, that is an ideal, and we live in the real world. Sometimes, compromises have to be made.

Take heart and know that almost all businesses exist to help people solve their problems. Whether you are picking up the trash or figuring out a better way to transfer information using lasers, all businesses work because there is a need for their product or services. If you can approach your work with an eye on not only solving the problem at hand, but doing so in a way that improves the well-being of the society we live in, bonus!

Your Community

Next up is the community in which you live. If you do not make improving your community a priority, your decisions will not reflect that. Here is a little tip, improving the community in which you live benefits you. Consider this an enlightened self-interest issue.

You are dependent on the community in which you live for support, food, security, and more. If you pollute the stream everyone drinks from because you put your business first and did not bother to consider the impact you would have on your community because you do not think improving your community is one of your responsibilities; all you have really done is poison the drinking water you and your family relies on! Not too bright.

While you may not always be able to take constructive action to improve your community, you can always make sure you do not cause your community any harm. Prioritize your community in order to make decisions that benefit your community and do not cause harm. A flourishing community is a community you can flourish in.

The World in Which You Live

Finally, we have a responsibility to improve the world in which we all live. You are not the only human out of the seven billion plus humans that matter. Additionally, our planet earth is actually our space ship. Our survival depends completely on whether our earth is healthy or not. We all need clean food, air, and water at a minimum, if we are to survive.

Do not choose actions that will cause harm to the earth as that will negatively impact you as well. If you can do something to help alleviate the pain and suffering of some of your fellow humans, you should do that, too. This is all part of what it means to be an active and involved citizen of the world.

What makes a Humanist a Humanist is that we consider all of our fellow humans worthy of the same compassion, dignity, and concern that we give to ourselves and our immediate family. Yes, we prioritize the well-being of ourselves and our family, but that does not mean we abandon our responsibilities to others. This is all about finding balance. To balance things properly, make finding balance a priority.

The goal of a humanist is to live life fully, love other people, and make the world a better place. We believe that the way we flourish as individuals is when we actively care for the well-being of others. And, the best way to care for others is to create societies and organizations in which anyone and everyone can flourish.

How This Applies to Humanistic Business Management

What does all of this mean for someone interested in humanistic business management? It means that, when you consider your business and business problems, you view it through the lens of helpfulness.

Business is not an isolated selfish endeavor. When done right, it helps people and helps solve their and our problems. When you focus, not just on what you can extract from a business, but on how your business and your work can help make the world a better place; it transforms your approach.

Business is not just about making money. It is about doing good in the world. How can you best balance the needs of your day-to-day business against the need to not pollute our world? How can you best balance the need to provide a living for your family while at the same time making sure that your employees can do the same?

The humanistic business management approach replaces the greed motive with a more balanced and humane work ethic. You do not have to abandon profits to do good in the world. In fact, doing good for the sake of doing good will help you create a thriving business, one you can be proud of, that will truly make a positive difference in the world. You can do this while ensuring that you and your employees achieve a good work–life balance while doing work that is important and meaningful precisely because you are helping to make the world better. This approach also creates customers who not only need your products and services, but who will also buy in to the overall mission of your company, which is to make the world a better place.

Let me give you some real-life examples of companies that have taken this approach. Both of these examples are from the world of agriculture and food.

Example 1: The Coalition of Immokalee Farmworkers (CIW)

I live in Florida, specifically in an area that is home to four tomato-processing plants. In the past 15 years, we have had nine slavery convictions here because some of the tomato farmers were using enslaved labor. Still.

It is because of the work of an activist farm workers group known as the Coalition of Immokalee Farmworkers (CIW) (http://ciw-online.org) that these cases were investigated and tried. Additionally, the CIW has led the way in creating a fair food framework to eradicate the abuse of farmworkers. By advocating for a penny per pound increase in pay for tomato farmers, and for an ethical framework for companies who buy tomatoes (restaurants, supermarkets, and the like), to help monitor conditions in the fields and report abuses, they changed the business practices of tomato farmers in Florida for the better. The good news is that the CIW was successful, and we have not had a slavery trial here in six years.

While it may seem like an easy decision to pay 1 cent more per pound of tomatoes to help ensure that the people picking the tomatoes are not treated literally as slaves, there was resistance from business groups, specifically, the Florida Tomato Growers Exchange. Eventually, businesses that buy tomatoes agreed that they do not want slave tomatoes, and they want the people picking their tomatoes to be treated fairly and with dignity. The Florida tomato growers eventually agreed to the terms of the CIW Fair Food accord, and as of now, 90 percent of all tomatoes grown in Florida are grown under the Fair Food accords, which include a penny per pound salary increase for the tomato pickers and a commitment to buy only from farmers who comply with the code of conduct.

In hindsight, it is amazing that any company resisted such reasonable requests. Do not buy from farmers who use enslaved labor, and please pay a penny more per pound to your workers for their work so they can have a living wage. Yet, it took the first company targeted four years to agree and nine years for the tomato farmers themselves to agree to stop using enslaved labor. Why the delay? Because the business people in question, like most people, are resistant to change, and they were not thinking strategically or compassionately. They were looking at their bottom line and they were not all that concerned with the impact they were having on others. They were focused on their immediate business and did not extend their focus of concern to the well-being of the workers in their supply chain because they were not their direct employees. The fact that there was a slavery problem in the supply chain just was not one of their main concerns.

A humanistic business manager takes a different approach. If we were to learn that one of our suppliers is using enslaved labor, we do our research to verify that this is true, and if it is, find out how prevalent the problem is and then we take steps to ensure that our suppliers comply with our demands that our products are not produced using enslaved labor. Why? Because slavery is an abhorrent practice, and *no one* should be subjected to it ever and, certainly, not in our name. We know that our companies will be fine if we pay a little bit more for our raw goods in order to ensure that the very real humans that make our business possible are treated fairly and with dignity.

It is a reasonable thing to do and it is going to happen eventually, so why not be on the right side of these sorts of conflicts and side with the workers instead of siding with the folks that claim respecting basic human rights is going to drive them out of business? None of the companies that changed their practices have gone out of business!!!! None. They just claimed they would to excuse their horrendous business practices.

This is all about balance. All the companies participating in the Fair Food accord are doing fine economically. Enslaved labor and poor working conditions were and are not necessary to run a profitable business. They are only necessary if you are running a greedy business. Do not be greedy. Make sure your commitment to corporate social responsibility is real and not just a marketing ploy. Make sure your decisions include the well-being of everyone your business interacts with from employees, to contractors to customers and vendors.

The other lesson we can learn is from the approach the CIW took. The CIW was successful because their strategy was both strategic and realistic and based in a profound understanding of humanistic management and change management.

They did not try to fix the entire farming industry at once. They did not demonize the companies that they targeted or the people running them. Instead, they targeted a single crop and a single purchaser of that crop, and they made a very reasonable and modest proposal that would be impossible for any rational human to refuse. This proposal, as modest as it was, was holistic, meaning that it affected the entire supply chain from worker to farmer to supplier to end user in a way that would fix the main problems facing farm workers (salary and working conditions). They approached all negotiations with the assumption that ultimately, these companies would decide to do the right thing, and that everyone would benefit from making this change. They understood and planned for the resistance to change that they encountered.

By all metrics, their strategy has been successful. We have not had a slavery trial here in years, and the CIW is more focused on slavery prevention than prosecution these days. They have shifted their energies to the enforcement of their agreements, as well as working on the straggler companies who have yet to sign the fair food accords and expanding their impact beyond Florida.

The importance of utilizing reality-based problem-solving and compassionate strategic thinking cannot be overstated. The lessons of humanistic business management are not limited to the world of business. They work just as well in the non-profit sector because, ultimately, this is about managing people, making good decisions, and succeeding at your goals.

Example 2: Slave-Free Chocolate

The other example is also from agriculture, and it is from the chocolate industry. Most chocolate is grown in a fair food style. However, chocolate farmers in Ghana and the Ivory Coast are notorious for using enslaved child labor. Whenever you hear of child slave ships off Africa not being allowed to go into a port somewhere, it is related to the use of children as slaves on chocolate farms in Africa. Please understand that when I say child slave labor, I am talking about 11- and 12-year-old boys being forced to work on these farms, and eventually dying of malnutrition and lack of health care when they get injured.

The solution to this problem is simple; companies that make chocolate should refuse to buy chocolate from those countries that use enslaved labor unless they can verify that their chocolate is slave-free. This is fairly easy to do because there are so many other sources of chocolate that do not enslave children in this way. Major chocolate manufacturers still refuse to certify that their chocolate is slave-free and have fought against legislation to ensure their products do not contain chocolate farmed by enslaved children. They get around this by purchasing chocolate blends so that it is impossible to know where the chocolate came from before it is imported into the United States.

Enter the organic and slave-free chocolate companies. There are at least 27 by last count that certify their chocolate is fair farmed and slave-free. Where there is a problem, there is a solution. Businesses that provide those solutions in ethical ways can not only thrive, they are often major catalysts of change.

The fair-trade slave-free chocolate companies provide an ethical alternative to the major chocolate brands and are spearheading a new way of doing business by making fair trade, fair labor, and sustainable farming a priority in their business. These companies are doing all this profitably. They are doing good creating a product that is admittedly a luxury product, but by doing so, they are changing the way business is done and creating a new economic model that is not only sustainable and ethical, and profitable at the same time. Eventually, even the big businesses will follow suit.

Even Walmart has committed to making organic farming profitable, and they are changing how big supermarkets source their food as a result. All it took was a commitment to make it happen.

The idea that making a profit requires you to harden your heart against suffering is nonsense! It is a rationalization made by greedy psychopaths who lack compassion, and we should not hesitate to state so plainly and reject these sorts of callous rationalizations.

Humanistic business managers refuse to make that sort of compromise and refuse to coddle the psychopaths who do. You can be ethical, compassionate, and responsible and run a good and profitable business at the same time. By choosing this path, you will not only find that you are living your life consistently with your values but that your life and your work are infused with meaning and purpose as well.

There is no need to compromise your values in business. Do not succumb to temptation. Do not believe psychopaths that tell you that harming people is OK. It is not. Make it your responsibility to figure out a way to do good and be good in your business at the same time.

Success Redefined

The goal of a Humanist is to lead a happy and fulfilling life. To lead happy fulfilling lives, we need to properly balance our personal and professional lives. We also need to find a way to infuse our lives with meaning so that we are not just biding our time here on earth.

If this was easy to do, we would all be doing it, and the self-help market would not exist. There is a reason why people have existential angst. Without some idea of why we are alive, our lives become meaningless.

This is not a new problem; it has existed throughout our time here on earth as humans. I find it interesting that the greatest teachers throughout history have all taught pretty much the same thing. The solution to this existential problem is to make being ethical a priority, to be compassionate with others and to work to make the world a better place for everyone and not only for a select few.

There is a reason why this formula for success, happiness, and fulfillment is always the same, regardless of who the teacher is. It works.

What Is Success?

Too often, we define success in material terms.

As individuals we are successful if we have a good job, or a new car or a new home. These are material definitions of success, and while achieving these things certainly gives us a certain sense of security, they usually only bring momentary happiness or pleasure. They do not help us achieve a lasting sense of fulfillment. Material definitions of success are flawed because they do not include well-being and flourishing in the definition of success.

We have the same problem with how we definite corporate success or governmental success. Corporations are judged by their balance sheets. Did they make a profit for the owners? What is not being asked is whether or not their employees are flourishing. Are customer's lives being made better? Is the company destroying the environment and polluting the commons we all rely on? I find it hard to believe that a company that cannot afford to pay employees a living wage and that has to rely on taxpayer assistance to support their employees, so the employees do not die of starvation would ever be considered successful. If you do not make enough money for your employees to survive, then your business is a failure. If you are flourishing as a business owner, but refuse to ensure that your employee's well-being is provided for, then you are a failure as a person.

We have the same problem with states and countries. We ask, what is the Gross Domestic Product (GDP), meaning, how much stuff have we created and built and how much wealth have we accumulated as a country. We do not ask how that wealth is distributed. We do not ask whether the people of the country have enough food, or whether they have clean water and adequate shelter. We do not ask whether the children and young people have access to education. We do not ask about the general health and well-being of the population.

A Humanist does not judge success solely on material wealth. We view material wealth as a means to an end. Success for us is judged by well-being. Are we taking care of each other? Does everyone in society have what they need to flourish or not?

We are not the only people who think this way. More and more people are using well-being as the metric by which we judge success.[3] These new metrics do not take wealth out of the equation, they just balance wealth with other indicators of societal well-being. The idea that we either create wealth or we care about well-being is a false dichotomy. We can very easily do both. The humanistic approach is to make well-being our moral good and we treat wealth as a means to achieve societal flourishing.

---

[3] http://oecd.org/officialdocuments/publicdisplaydocumentpdf/?cote=SDD/DOC(2018)7&docLanguage=En.

Ethics of Individual Success

If well-being and individual flourishing is our goal, then how do we make that happen? Material success can provide us with temporary feelings of success and contentment. But, to make the feeling of contentment stay and take root, we need to define success in a different way. This is why, most teachers and philosophers advocate that you define success in terms of how well you live your ethics.

When you make being ethical your primary goal in life, you find that it is not only fairly easy to achieve, it is also something that brings great satisfaction when you do. It is when I am reaching out to help others in need that I find my greatest satisfaction. It is in those moments that I finally feel centered and alive and like I am doing what I am supposed to be doing. That is why, being ethical is the primary goal in pretty much every religion and major philosophy.

The other benefit of defining your success by how well you live your ethics is that this is an ongoing goal. You can never really be finished with it because every day and every interaction requires you to live up to your ethical ideals. It is deeply satisfying precisely because you are never finished with it. There is no let down *'now what do I do'* feeling, of the sort you get when your goals are more material in nature.

Plus, the more you do this, the better you get at it, and the more satisfied you become. The sense of contentment and happiness and feelings of being successful that comes with practicing ethics is so incredible; you will find that your desire to define success in material terms is diminished.

Do not get me wrong, material success is important. I strive for it every day. It just is not the only thing I strive for. What is more important to me is being the best most ethical person I can be, regardless of what else happens. I do a fairly good job at this, and because knowing I am doing my best to be that good person I want to be is so satisfying, I have been as happy during the lean times in my life as I have been in times of plenty.

How you define success matters. Do not define success in a shallow material way. Define it in terms of the sort of human being you wish to be. Make it your priority to be that person and enjoy the success when you do.

This is a transformative way to think about who you are and why you are and what you want out of life. Do not deny yourself the benefits of approaching life ethically.

What Brings Us Happiness?

Happiness is elusive. We all know we would prefer to be happy. Few of us really know how to be happy, so we chase pleasure instead. Pleasure is temporary. It does not last, so we chase more of it. This is one of the reasons why people spend so much time and energy chasing material success. They know it will help increase their pleasure, even if it does so temporarily.

Pleasure is like a drug. It wears off over time, and to keep that feeling, you try to get more. You cycle through periods of pleasure and withdraw, always seeking that next fix.

The smarter approach is to recognize the futility of that endless cycle and instead seek out a deeper and more meaningful approach to finding happiness. That more meaningful approach is to pay attention to the people in your life.

Think back to the times you felt the happiest and the most fulfilled. Chances are they involve a memory of spending time someone special. It probably was not a major event either. These memories are usually something simple and mundane. It is not all the accoutrements of the relationship; it is focusing on someone else that makes us feel happy and content.

Our greatest happiness comes from our relationships with others. This makes sense because we are social animals, so belonging and having that sense of belonging to someone else has a profound effect on us.

To be happy, nurture your relationships and make time for them. Do not take them for granted and tell yourself that you are taking time away from them to benefit them. That is a rationalization. Yes, sometimes it is necessary, but certainly not all the time. Find a way to balance your professional and personal life, and make your personal life a priority. Otherwise, you will get to the end of your life and wonder what it was all for.

The other aspect of finding happiness in others that is so important is the cultivation of compassion. In order to treat the people you love well and with dignity, it helps to have feelings of tenderness, love, and compassion for them.

Extending your feelings of love and compassion to the entirety of humanity is the next level of fulfillment. Your feelings of compassion help connect you to all life on earth. You are not alone in the universe. You only are alone if you are too selfish to reach out to other humans with love and compassion.

This is why, all the great teachers taught compassion for others. It is the key to happiness. When we feel compassion, we feel calm contentment, and that is reason enough to practice it. The real reason to practice and cultivate love and compassion for others is because it helps guide and nurture our relationships.

Our relationship with others *is* what brings us the most happiness and contentment in our lives. It is also through the active exercise of our compassion for others that we find meaning and purpose in our lives.

How Can We Be Fulfilled?

We humans do not do well unless we have a goal to strive for. We really do crave meaning and purpose. Without that, we are adrift. This is why we all suffer from existential angst to some extent. The cure for this angst, as taught by pretty much every major philosopher and religious leader throughout history, is to focus our work on making the world a better place, not just for ourselves, but for everyone else as well.

By taking on the responsibility to make the world better, to ease the suffering of others, and to help where you can, infuses life with meaning. You are no longer adrift, you have a purpose. And it is a good one!

Your time here on earth may be limited. If you are committed to not wasting it and doing your best to improve life for others, your life will be well spent. You will get to the end of your life and know that you did your best with what you had at your disposal. You will know that you did not waste your life.

Humanists, by and large, do not suffer from motivation problems. We accept that we cannot know for sure if our actions matter. We choose to act as if they do because, in the here and now, they do matter. My actions impact myself, my family, and the people whose lives I touch. That matters.

The fact that I have a limited time to live my life is also a huge motivator for me. I do not know if there is another life after this one. What I do know is that, if I do not live this one fully, I probably do not deserve another one. After all, if I waste this life by doing nothing of importance for humanity and the world and the people I care about then what business do I have living a second life. I would probably just waste that as well.

Committing yourself to making the world a better place and to easing the suffering of others is a powerful motivator. It is a goal that is worth pursuing, and by doing so, you will help provide your life with deep meaning and powerful purpose. There is no other goal you can find for yourself that will have such a tremendous impact on your life for the better. Do not deny yourself this.

This ethical approach is not just a personal approach. It applies to everything. Your business ethics should be the same as your personal ethics. When you apply this same philosophy to your business and work, the impact you have will be amazing. Do not deny yourself and the rest of us your compassion.

Putting it All Together

The Humanist approach to life and business is powerful.

- Be the best most ethical person you can be.
- Reach out to everyone you meet with compassion.
- Make it your life goal to make the world a better place.

You are already motivated to do this. You probably just need someone to give you permission to be that person and to nudge you to actually commit to being that person. Once you start, you will realize that this is not a chore. It is so intensely satisfying that you will wonder why you ever hesitated to make being a truly ethical person in all you do a priority.

Is it always easy? No. It requires constant practice. We are all human. We are all fallible. We all get frustrated at times. Further, we all have a tendency to allow our negative emotions to guide our thinking instead of using reason, logic, and compassion as our guide.

The desire to do good is the easy part. The hard part is learning to think more rationally so that your decisions and problem-solving help you achieve your noblest goals, instead of thwarting you. This is why, Humanists spend so much time honing our critical thinking skills.

Unless you are committed to doing your best to positively impact people in the here and now, you will not be motivated to do the hard work that is necessary to problem solve effectively.

Unless you are truly motivated by and practice compassion, your thinking and your problem-solving will be flawed because, instead of viewing other people as they really are, you will be viewing them through a distorted lens of your own making.

Unless you commit to being the best most ethical person in all that you do, you will not be motivated to treat the very real humans that inhabit your life and give your life meaning the dignity and compassion they deserve.

The Humanist approach is powerful because it is pragmatic, compassionate, ethical, and responsible. It is an approach that encourages us to live life fully and happily while working to make the world a better place for everyone to live in. Its methods and approach help us make better more ethical decisions. Its insistence on pragmatic reality-based problem solving helps us to be more effective and efficient.

This is an approach that will help you better confront the challenges of life and help you integrate your ethics and your business in a way that is both emotionally satisfying and economically successful.

It all starts with a choice. What choice will you make?

PART III

Problem-Solving Like a Humanist

CHAPTER 1

Introduction: Why Critical Thinking?

Humanism is not just about ethics. It is also a dedication to effective problem-solving. The reason we rely so heavily on science and reject supernaturalism is because we are dedicated to finding solutions that actually work and that are ethically sound at the same time.

Without dedicating ourselves to finding out what is really real, we cannot solve our problems, and our ethical reasoning will be flawed. For this reason, Humanists are committed to critical thinking.

This part of the book will help you learn how to answer the three most important questions for any strategy. What is your real problem? What is really causing it, and what will really work to solve it?

Discussion and Topics Covered

It does not matter what you want to do—a good strategy is important. Strategies help us know what we are working on, why we are working on it, and most importantly, how. Not all strategies are effective. To give yourself the best chance of success, it is important to take several steps to ensure that your strategy is reality based.

The following are topics that I will discuss in this section:

- One simple technique to ensure you focus on your real problem and not a proxy problem
- Six critical thinking skills necessary to ensure your strategy is reality based
- How to evaluate your alternatives scientifically

Keep in mind that this part of the book is meant to be a quick overview of reality-based processes and techniques used by Humanists. There are concepts I will only introduce, but not get into their detail. Learning how to think critically is a life-long endeavor.

CHAPTER 2

Strategic Planning 101

Let us start by defining what we are talking about. A strategy is not a goal, it is the way you plan to get to your goal.

If you are going to the supermarket, there are probably many ways you can get there. You choose a route, and you go. The route is the strategy. Where you are going is the goal. But, there is something else you need and that is a reason to go. No one just wants to go to the store. They go to the store for a reason. Do not develop a strategy without knowing the reason (the real reason) you are doing it. This is the most important part of any strategy and it is amazing how many people get this part wrong. The reason they get it wrong is because it seems obvious, but it is not. They do not know why they are doing it, they just think they need to. People go to the supermarket all the time and forget what they went there to get. Do not make this mistake in business.

Let us assume you have a goal and you know why you want to achieve that goal. Now you want to create a strategy to get there. To succeed, you need a *healthy* dose of reality! It does not matter if you know why you want to go to the supermarket; if you do not take into account reality, you probably will not make it there. It may seem silly when discussing going to the supermarket, but things happen, such as accidents, that block the road that can prevent you from getting to your destination.

If you think you can just go straight there—in a straight line, A to B—you might find that there are houses in your way. Understanding what is in your way and what you need to do to get around them to get to your destination is very important if you are actually going to get there. Reality really does matter even for simple strategies. The more complex the strategy, the more important it is to base it in reality.

CHAPTER 3

Reality-Based Decision-Making

There are several aspects of problem-solving that can benefit from taking a reality-based approach. One question that we should ask is, what is your real problem? The main way people go wrong in strategy development is they try to solve the wrong problem, or worse, a problem that they do not actually have! I call these proxy problems. These are problems that stand in for your real problem but are not your real problem. Any time you spend time, energy, and money on proxy problems is time, energy, and money not spent on fixing your real problem.

Assuming that you know what your real problem is, the next place people go off course is they do not know what is really causing their problem. They guess, and guess wrong. Instead of fixing the underlying cause, they work on something that will have zero impact on their problem. This happens quite frequently. Again, if you are spending time, energy, and money on things that are not going to solve your real problem, you are wasting time, energy, and money.

Finally, it is not enough to know what your real problem is and what is really causing it, if you do not know what will really work to solve it. As I mentioned earlier, there are a lot of ways to go from A to B. Some routes will get you to your destination and some will not. You need to put effort into finding out which ones will really work and which ones really do not if you want to be successful.

CHAPTER 4

Six Necessary Critical Thinking Skills

To develop a realistic strategy, find out what is real and what is not. The best way to do that is to get in the habit of thinking critically.

There are six basic critical thinking skills that will help you learn what is real and what is not. Here is a list of the necessary skills so that you can start learning them.

First, *analyze* your problem! Ask yourself why! Just being willing to question your assumptions will go a long way toward making sure your strategy is reality based. In fact, the question *why*, is the single most important question you can ask. What is your real problem and what is really causing it? And, *why* do you want to solve it? That is two-thirds of a successful strategy right there. The remaining critical thinking skills will help you figure out what will really work to solve it. Get in the habit of asking yourself *why*. I am going to go into a lot more detail on exactly how *why* works in the next chapter.

The next skill you need to learn is *freethought*. Freethought is to think critically, yet freely. It is a form of brainstorming. The easiest way to do this is by considering at least three options.

We all tend to think in terms of black or white. But, if you remember that sometimes things are gray, you will be way ahead of the game. Again, I am going to discuss exactly how to apply this skill in another chapter, once we start talking about how to figure out the root cause of your problem.

Another skill is doing *research*. Research will help you learn what is really causing your problem and what might really work to solve it. You need to research what does not work in addition to what will. If you think you have a solution that might work, look for evidence that it does not work. It is necessary to see both sides. Do not just look at the evidence that a vendor gives you and say, "Wow, that looks like it works." Find out if it really does work before spending money on it!

This is why *doubt and skepticism* are such important critical thinking skills and why scientists and skeptics are always debunking things. A lot of people think of doubt and skepticism as negative thinking habits. They are actually really optimistic habits to have. People who doubt, believe they can solve their problems; they just do not want to be duped into spending money, time, and resources on things that do not work.

Doubt and skepticism are not enough. In order to know what is true or not, we must be able to evaluate the evidence. This requires a skill called *scientific literacy*. People who are scientifically literate know how to read and understand research papers. They do not have to take someone's word for it; they can evaluate the evidence presented and make a determination on whether the research is valid or not. This skill can be taught, and it is probably the most important skill to have in the modern age.

There are all sorts of claims about what is good and what is bad for you. Knowing what is fake and what is scientifically valid can save your life. People die all of the time from preventable diseases because they put their faith in *alternative* medicine, which is medicine that has no scientific evidence to support it.

The final critical thinking skill everyone should learn is how to identify *logical fallacies*.

Just because one thing is true does not mean what comes next is also true. Learning what fallacies are and how to identify them will help you determine whether what follows is valid and true, or not. What I recommend is that you go online and type in *fallacy* and start reading the lists that people have posted online to begin understanding more.

CHAPTER 5

Proxy Problems and How to Avoid Them

Let us focus on our first task, which is making sure that we are at least focused on solving our real problem, and not a proxy problem.

Albert Einstein, a member of the First Humanist Society of NY, once said that, if he had one hour to solve a problem, he would spend 50 minutes defining the problem. I cannot stress enough how important it is that you make sure you are solving your real problem and not a proxy problem. The way to avoid proxy problems is to ask yourself *why*. Why do I want to solve *this* problem?

For example, let us say I am a farmer, and that my plants are not growing due to a drought and I would really like it to rain. To solve my problem, I need to ask myself some questions. Why do I want it to rain? Answer? So I can get water on my field. Why do I want to get water on my field? So my plants will grow. Why do I want my plants to grow? So I have something to eat in order to not die of starvation.

As soon as you get to the bad thing that will happen if you do not do whatever it is, you have found your real problem. In this example, our real problem is that we want our plants to grow. To grow, they need water and sunlight. Sunlight happens without much worry. Water is more problematic? That is our real problem. How do we get water on our field?

Where people go wrong is that they lose sight of the real problem because they are instead focusing on a potential solution to the problem to the exclusion of all other possible solutions. They start thinking, I need it to rain so I can get water on my field. How do I make it rain? Do not turn a potential solution into a proxy problem. In other words, a problem that you think will solve your real problem, but that is not your real problem.

Understanding not only what it is you ultimately are trying to accomplish, and what happens if you do not, is very motivating! In this case, I need my plants to grow or I will die.

Make sure you consider all of the different ways you might solve the problem. If you are focused on only one of your potential solutions, you are ignoring and not exploring your other possible options, which might be better. Consider all your options so that you do not end up missing opportunities that are almost always easier and more effective.

Finally, proxy problems are often not solvable. You cannot make it rain. Civilizations have literally collapsed trying to make it rain. Avoid making this mistake. Figure out what your real problem is and focus on solving it.

CHAPTER 6

Root Causes and Real Problems

Let us assume you did your work and you asked yourself *why*, and you are pretty sure that you are focusing on your real problem, and not on a proxy problem that you think is important. Now you need to find out what is really causing your problem. To do this, you need to ask a lot of questions.

Why is this happening? How does it happen? Am I sure this information is correct?

To succeed, you need to be willing to ask questions, do some research, and evaluate the science behind it. Do not assume that you know why something is happening.

To help, I am going to introduce you to a critical thinking trick I like to call "The Rule of Threes." This is a mental shortcut that I use to help me make sure I am engaging in freethought, and that I consider all of the possibilities.

I was taught this by my boss at a tower company I used to work at. It turned out that everything we did could be broken down into three options. For instance, if you need access to land in order to put a tower on it, you could purchase the land, lease it, or get an easement onto it. You have at least three options. Most people think you can just purchase land or lease/rent land. There is actually a third option. The people who take the time to think of the third scenario are usually the ones that figure out how to creatively, effectively, and economically solve their problems.

Notice that I said my problem is that I need access to use land, not that I need land. Needing land is a proxy problem. Needing to access the land was the real problem we had. The difference is minor, but it is the difference between a successful strategy and a more costly strategy. Any money we did not spend on acquiring access to land was money we could spend on something else.

The reason I want you to think of at least three options is because, all humans, myself included, tend to think in terms of dichotomies. We can either eat-in or go out. You are either with us or against us. People who work in marketing use this tendency of ours, all the time, to trick us into thinking we need their product. Either you buy that cord-organizing piece of plastic or you cannot possibly use anything else to wire up your television and sound system. They intentionally leave out alternatives. Do not fall into this trap.

The Rule of Three: Possible Causes

The first way to use the rule of three is to think of at least three possible causes for our problem. Once you can think of three, you can think of four or five. The reason to do this is to make sure that you do not default to your assumptions about root causes. Once you have a bunch of possible causes, figure out which ones are actually real and are actually impacting your real problem.

Once I have done my brainstorming, I narrow down my list to the three that I think are most likely true. I then do my research and ask myself, what do I know about this and what do I *not* know? What does the science say?

For example, let us talk about the subject of bullying. We know we want to stop bullying because it causes so much long-term harm to kids. What causes bullying? Do you know? Or, do you just think you know? One of the reasons the bullying problem has been so difficult to solve is because people make a lot of assumptions about root causes. Is it bad parents? Mental illness? Sociopath? Enabled? Inherently evil?

One of the ways to tell that people are either working on a proxy problem or that they do not really know what is causing their problem is that they fail to solve the problem.

In the case of bullying, science tells us that it is a learned behavior, meaning it is rewarded. Good parents can produce bullying children because parenting has very little to do with it. Shocking, I know. The point is, until we start focusing on the real root cause of our problem, we will not solve it!

Be skeptical about what you think the causes of your problems are. Think of at least three possible causes, or more, then use research and science to figure out which of your possible causes are real and which ones are just assumptions. Do not spend time on proxy problems or proxy causes.

CHAPTER 7

Real Solutions to Real Problems

Let us assume that you are working on creating a solution to your real problem, and that you understand what is really causing it. Now what? You now need a solution that will positively impact the real root cause of your real problem so that you can fix it.

We are going to use the rule of three again. We are going to consider at least three possible solutions to our problem. We are not going to go with the first person who comes along and offers us a solution. We are going to look for solutions that really do work to impact the real root cause of our problem. Once we have researched potential solutions, we are going to narrow our focus down to the three solutions that are most likely to work. Spend time properly defining your problem, and the rest becomes much easier.

We know what our real problem is, so we will not get side-tracked on interesting, but pointless, proxy problems. We know what we need to do to solve our problem because we figured out what is really causing it. This helps us narrow down potential solutions to things that will actually have a decent chance of working. We are not looking for solutions that solve proxy problems, and we are also not looking for solutions to assumed causes. We are looking for real solutions to the real causes of our real problems.

I always like to narrow down my possible solutions to three and then do a side-by-side comparison to choose the best one. Sticking to my rule of three, I have three criteria by which I judge potential solutions:

1. It is focused on solving the root cause of my real problem.
2. It has real science to back it up, meaning it actually works and is not just a placebo solution.

3. Is it cost effective and easy to implement, given the real resources at my disposal.

This last bit is important because, if it costs more than I can afford, or it takes more resources than I have at my disposal, it will not work because I will not be able to implement it.

Example

I run an online business selling online courses. I have several problems running my company. I need to have a way for people to register for courses. I need to accept payment; otherwise, I will not get paid. And, I need to make sure people who sign up are registered into my online course system.

One potential solution is to do it manually. Have people write me or call me and send me a check, at which point I manually place them in the course. That would work, but it is time consuming and slow, and not an ideal solution.

A second option is I can automate things. I can use online forms to capture the information and online payment systems to allow people to pay online when they register. I can use scripts to automatically transfer that information into a format that I can use to upload the weekly registrations into my course system. This will work, and it will save time and is fairly cost effective.

A third option is I can pay someone to do it for me. In fact, there is an online system that I can purchase that would do all of this for me and would integrate into my website quite well. That system costs more than 10,000 U.S. dollars. Not exactly easy money to find when you are a startup. But, it is certainly an option.

If I wanted, I could add a 4th or 5th option like hiring someone. But, to make a choice on which is best, I take my three best options based on my three main criteria and make a decision from there.

In this case, all three of my options will solve my real problem and all three will really work. The deciding factor is: Can I really implement it?

I chose option two, to set up automations to make it work. It is a little more time consuming than having someone else do it, but it is way more cost effective. The time it takes is about three hours per week. I now have a solution that really solves my problem, is cost effective, and makes good use of the real resources at my disposal. A reality-based strategy that really works. Success!

CHAPTER 8

Examples

In this chapter, I will provide examples of these techniques in order to give a little bit more perspective on how this really works when developing a strategy.

Effective reality-based strategies take into account the following:

- *The real problem* that really needs to be solved
- *The real root causes* of that problem
- *Real solutions* that will have a real impact on the root causes
- *Really achievable*, that is, I have the resources required to create that impact

Example of a Proxy Problem

An example of a *proxy problem* comes from the climate change debate. While I was teaching a course in Socratic Jujutsu, otherwise known as how to win arguments without arguing, one of my students wanted to know how to convince people climate change is human-caused. I asked her, why do you want to do that? Why does it matter whether people think it is caused by humans or not? I used why questions to help her identify her real problem.

She said she wanted people to agree that climate change is caused by humans, so they would adopt the policy changes she thinks are needed. Asking her *why* helped her understand that getting people to agree that climate change is caused by humans was not her real problem. It was a proxy problem. It is one of many possible solutions to her real problem. Her real problem was the getting the policy changes she wanted adopted. There are a multitude of ways to get policies enacted. But, as long as she was focused on getting consensus on it being human-caused, she was not working on getting policy enacted at all. She was focused on a proxy problem and was not understanding why her efforts were not bearing legislative fruit.

It does not matter what problem you want to solve; if you do not take the time to question your assumptions about that problem, you will probably end up wasting time, energy, and money trying to fix a proxy problem. Stripping away extraneous and irrelevant information helps you focus on what really matters. Whether you are trying to get into a new market, figuring out your hiring needs, or entering into some sort of contract, being super clear about what you really need to accomplish will help you not get distracted by extraneous proxy problems that do not impact anything.

Example of a Real Root Cause Problem

An example of a *root cause problem* is bullying. What causes bullying? We know that we want bullying to stop, and it is easy to articulate why. But, what causes the bully to bully? Bad parents? Mental illness? General levels of evilness?

Those are all assumptions. Choose one without finding out if it is true and you will fail to stop bullying. If you have not read my work on bullying, I am about to blow your mind.

It does not matter why a bully is bullying. It is irrelevant to getting them to stop.

Wanting to know why they bully is a proxy problem. I realize that the question of why does a bully bully, has the word *why* in it. But, we need to ask the question, "Why do we want to know why a bully bullies?" The answer is because we want them to stop! We think that, if we know why they bully, we can get them to stop. Our real problem is we want them to stop. That is the problem we should be focusing our energies on.

Always ask yourself why you are focusing on something to get to your real root problem.

Once we focus on the fact that we want them to stop, we can focus on how to get them to stop. Knowing why they bully is in service to that goal of getting them to stop. It is one possible way to approach this problem—but not the only way. Focusing on it—to the exclusion of other possible approaches—has caused us as a society to fail. I am not going to get into the science here because I have written about it elsewhere. But, science tells us that people bully because they are rewarded for it. If we want it to stop, we need to stop rewarding it. A strategy to make a bully stop must focus on removing their reward to be successful. Now that we know that, we are in a position to look for solutions that will help us stop rewarding bullies.

A realistic assessment of your real problem and the real root causes of your problem are the foundation upon which a realistic and effective strategy is built.

And again, this technique of questioning your assumptions will help you regardless of the problem you have. Why aren't your customers re-enrolling? Why are you paying so much overtime? Why did your energy costs triple? Do not assume you know the answer. Question your assumption and find out.

Example of a Real Solution That Has a Real Impact

An example of a *real solution problem* comes from change management.

There are several possible reasons why attempts to create change fail:

- The proposed solution does not work.
- The proposed solution is a fix for a proxy problem that does not really exist. In other words, we succeed at changing behavior, but it does not impact anything. The original problem is still there because the strategy was designed to fix a proxy problem.
- The proposed solution does work, but the people pushing for adoption do not know how to effectively create behavioral change so that the solution is adopted.

There are more possible reasons why change management strategies fail, but I will leave this at three for now.

I actually teach change management using a behavioral science perspective. Most of the change management failures I witness are because the person in charge of the process does not actually know how to change a person's behavior using behavioral science.

There really is a science to behavioral change, and it is directly applicable to all change management attempts. Knowing this science will help you manage the change processes more successfully. But if you do not even know you need to know this, you may just bumble along hoping for the best. That is not a good strategy.

To be effective at creating change, we should make sure that our attempted changes are focused on our real problem, and not a proxy problem. We should make sure that the change will actually fix things and have a real impact on outcomes. And, we should make sure that we know how to help our staff adjust to that change. Real problems. Real solutions. Real science. Real implementation.

Summary

To create a strategy that will work:

1. Focus on real problems, not proxy problems.
2. Find the real root cause of your problem using skepticism and science.
3. Research to find out what really works to solve the problem.
4. Make sure your strategy is really doable using the resources at your disposal.

PART IV

Case Studies

In this part of the book, we are going to look at a couple of problems that are vexing the business community, and that have defied solution for decades. The purpose of this is to consider how a humanist goes about solving real-world problems.

We use critical thinking to understand our problem. We use ethics to determine what a good outcome looks like and to understand why we should tackle this problem so that we are properly motivated to do the work necessary to solve the problem. And, we use science and reality-based problem-solving to actually fix it.

Because the focus of my work is how to use behavioral science to fix interpersonal problems, these case studies are focused on problems of harassment and diversity.

CHAPTER 1

Using Science, Humanism, and Technology to Finally Fix Our Harassment Problem

Question

Can we use science, ethical philosophy, and technology to finally fix the problem of harassment in the workplace?

Overview

Harassment in the workplace is a global problem. It negatively impacts productivity, well-being, diversity, ethical governance, and corporate culture. The social and economic cost of harassment in the workplace is so great that countries around the world mandate harassment training in the hopes that it will fix the problem. Despite all our efforts at education, the problem persists. Our failure is a good indication that we are trying to fix a proxy problem. It is time we take a different approach.

Behavioral scientists have known for decades how to extinguish unwanted behavior. This knowledge can and should be applied to the problem of abusive workplace behaviors. The technique required to get unwanted behavior to stop is easy to teach and learn. Our challenge is to change what we teach and how we teach it so the education we provide actually works to fix the problem.

I will first review the global nature of the problem and review the impact of abusive workplace behavior on human development and participation in society, as well as its impact on employee well-being. Why should we solve it is an ethical question.

I will then review the behavioral conditioning techniques required to extinguish unwanted behavior and how to apply this to bullying and harassment situations paying special attention to the retaliation dynamic. Finally, the educational challenges of dealing with harassment in the workplace will be discussed by reviewing existing educational efforts, the behavioral science reasons why those efforts fail, and how to get better results by integrating behavioral psychology with humanistic philosophy combined with a healthy dose of enlightened self-interest.

Harassment Causes Real Harm

Sexual harassment is in the news a lot. Powerful men are being exposed as serial harassers. Their companies, it turns out, have been spending a lot of money to "fix" the problem. Fix is the wrong word for what they are doing as they do not really fix the problem, they just pay someone to not talk about the problem.

Anita Hill, who was one of the first public figures in America to speak openly about harassment in the workplace, wrote an essay in response to the Harvey Weinstein scandal.[1] She asked, what if we treated harassment like we treat embezzlement? Imagine if instead of rumors being that he had sexually assaulted people, that the rumors were that he was embezzling funds. How would his board have responded differently?

The cost to society of allowing harassment to continue is immense. Not only is it costly to businesses to pay out on harassment claims, the quality of the work being done suffers, as effective problem-solving is nearly impossible when individuals with knowledge relevant to the problem are not allowed to contribute to problem-solving.

There is also the problem of lost productivity, which is the money spent to pay employees to work around the problem instead of fixing it. The Australian government estimates that bullying costs the Australian economy over 36 billion U.S. dollars a year in lost productivity.[2]

---

[1] Anita, H. 2018. "Women Face Creeps like Harvey Weinstein Everywhere—not Just in Hollywood." Retrieved from http://nydailynews.com/opinion/women-face-pigs-harvey-weinstein-anita-hill-article-1.3563555

[2] Potter, R.E., M.F. Dollard, and M.R. Tuckey. 2016. "Bullying and Harassment in Australian Workplaces." Retrieved from https://safeworkaustralia.gov.au/system/files/documents/1705/bullying-and-harassment-in-australian-workplaces-australian-workplace-barometer-results.pdf

Places where harassment flourishes have higher employee turnover, more sick days and other problems. Harassment in the workplace is bad for employee well-being, and it is bad for the bottom line.

Additionally, decision-making should be a rational process. If bullying and harassment are allowed to flourish, then decisions are being made by whoever has the most power, as opposed to what is best for the organization or project. A harassment or bullying dynamic has a negative cascading impact on the quality of work being done throughout an organization.

The Global Nature of the Problem

Harassment is a global problem affecting companies all over the world. A paper published in 2013 in the *Journal of Business Research* documented what they called "counter productive workplace behavior" on six continents.[3] While they found bullying occurs everywhere, they found that some countries and cultures tolerate it more than others.

Bullying and harassment in the workplace is of global concern. In total, 152 counties currently have laws prohibiting gender discrimination in the workplace, but only 122 provide legal protection against sexual harassment, leaving a full 68 countries (or approximately 235 million women) with no legal protection against sexual harassment.[4] There are clearly gaps in legislation that need to be filled.

Among the countries that do provide legal protection against sexual harassment, some require employers to provide training to prevent

---

[3] Power, J.L., C.M. Brotheridge, J. Blenkinsopp, L. Bowes-Sperry, N. Bozionelos, Z. Buzády, and S.M. Madero. 2013. "Acceptability of Workplace Bullying: A Comparative Study on Six Continents." Retrieved from https://sciencedirect.com/science/article/pii/S0148296311002955

[4] World Policy Analysis Center. 2017. "Preventing Gender-based Workplace Discrimination and Sexual Harassment: New Data on 193 Countries." Retrieved from https://worldpolicycenter.org/sites/default/files/WORLD%20Discrimination%20at%20Work%20Report.pdf

harassment in the workplace. For instance, the United States,[5] Canada,[6] Japan,[7] India,[8] the United Kingdom,[9] and Australia[10] all have laws making harassment illegal and mandating training to prevent harassment in the workplace. Some states go further. In California, employers must not only provide a sexual harassment training, they also must provide specific information on how to prevent abusive workplace behavior in general and information specific to gender identity harassment.

Changing the Educational Paradigm

What is obvious is that all of the laws and all the training being done because of these laws has not fixed the problem. *Harvard Business Review* in November 2015 acknowledged that training programs and reporting systems are not ending harassment.[11] Our challenge is to figure out what will.

---

[5] EEOC. 2018. "Harassment." Retrieved from https://eeoc.gov/laws/types/harassment.cfm

[6] Cision. 2017. "Government of Canada takes Strong Action against Harassment and Sexual Violence at Work." Retrieved from https:// newswire.ca/news-releases/government-of-canada-takes-strong-action-against-harassment-and-sexual-violence-at-work-655851813.html

[7] Freehills, H.S. LLP. 2015. "Japan: Sexual Harassment and Discrimination." Retrieved from https://lexology.com/library/detail.aspx?g=fb22c2ca-b6e7-471c-9690-6fb8c64c0bfa

[8] Dr. Shreeranjan. 2013. "India Ministry of Women and Child Development Notification." Retrieved from http://iitbbs.ac.in/notice/sexual-harrasment-of-women-act-and-rules-2013.pdf

[9] ACAS, UK Government. 2018. "Workplace Bullying and Harassment." Retrieved from https://gov.uk/workplace-bullying-and-harassment

[10] Australian Human Rights Commission. 2009. "Workplace Discrimination, Harassment and Bullying." Retrieved from https://humanrights.gov.au/employers/good-practice-good-business-factsheets/workplace-discrimination-harassment-and-bullying

[11] Dobbin, F., and A. Kalev. 2017. "Training Programs and Reporting Systems Won't End Sexual Harassment. Promoting More Women Will." Retrieved from https://hbr.org/2017/11/training-programs-and-reporting-systems-wont-end-sexual-harassment-promoting-more-women-will

Human behavior seems to be intractable in this area. Some people bully and use their power to harass and assault others. The good news is that behavioral scientists have known for decades how to stop unwanted behavior. It is time we put that knowledge to use.

Behavioral psychologists not only figured out how learning and unlearning occurs, they developed protocols, known as operant conditioning, decades ago to create behavioral change. One of these protocols is a technique to cause behavioral extinction, or the unlearning of an unwanted behavior. A Google Scholar search on the term behavioral extinction yields over 429,000 results,[12] all of which say the same thing.

To stop an unwanted behavior, remove the reward. This will cause the animal to escalate their behavior in an attempt to reclaim their reward. If the reward continues to be withheld, eventually, the animal will stop doing the behavior after a period of extreme behavior displays known as extinction burst or a blowout. All behavioral extinction in every animal ever studied (including humans), follows this pattern. There are no counter-examples. This is considered established science.

Our knowledge of what the behavioral extinction process entails and how to cause behavioral extinction to occur has important policy implications for how we approach the problem of bullying and harassment in the workplace and in society.

We know that any attempt to remove the reward received by a bully or a harasser will cause behavioral escalation, which in a harassment/bullying situation usually manifests as some form of retaliation. This is predicted to occur, and any program designed to stop harassment or bullying should take this fact into account.

Taking a behavioral approach to harassment also has implications for education. What are we teaching? Who we are teaching it to? Why are we teaching it to them? And, how we are teaching it all needs to be re-examined in light of the science.

---

[12] Google Scholar Search. 2018. "Behavioral Extinction." Retrieved from https://scholar.google.com/scholar?hl=en&as_sdt=0%2C10&q=behavioral+extinction&btnG=&oq=behavior

Current harassment curriculum appears to have adverse effects[13] and negative consequences on the people trained, including increased incidences of women being excluded in the workplace as males try to avoid harassment problems altogether. What we are currently doing is not working.

A Humanist Approach to the Problem

For ethical and practical reasons, Humanists want bullying and harassment to stop. Not only is it harmful to the individuals who experience it, it is also bad for society and bad for business. For both ethical and pragmatic reasons, we need to fix this problem.

The question is, how? For that, we need science to understand what causes bullying behavior and how to stop it. Science provides us with answers to both questions. People harass others, because it works. They get a reward. Science also tells us how to make it stop using operant conditioning techniques.

The science of how we create behavioral extinction as it applies to harassment behavior should be integrated into our legal structure, our training programs, and our management approaches.

Our goal should be to provide training that integrates behavioral science into the training and provide it to the people most motivated to learn it.

Creating a Strategy to Stop Harassment

Any strategy to fix a harassment problem must take into account not only how to make it stop, but also what resources are required.

Companies are already compelled to provide sexual harassment training to their employees. There are resources already being dedicated to this.

---

[13] Bingham and Scherer. 2001. "The Unexpected Effects of a Sexual Harassment Educational Program." Retrieved from http://journals.sagepub.com/doi/abs/10.1177/0021886301372001

If we change what is being trained to incorporate behavioral science, we should be able to have a positive impact on the problem.

Why the Current Training Programs Do Not Work and How to Fix Them

The current training mandates contain an assumption. The assumption is that the way to stop harassment is to convince the harasser to stop. The trainings are aimed at managers. They almost exclusively consist of legal reasons why harassing people is bad. In other words, it is illegal, do not do it. The assumption that scaring people with legal consequences will in any way change behavior is not grounded in science. We should not be surprised that these trainings not only do not cause serial harassers to have a change of heart, they also cause well-meaning people to be so scared; they overcompensate by excluding women in an effort to avoid legal consequences. We are seeing exactly the results one would expect from this sort of training.

We need to abandon the underlying assumption behind these legal trainings and get back to basics. We want the behavior to stop. To do that, we need to remove the reward. Where exactly is the reward coming from? And, how can we change the dynamic to remove it? And, can we do that with training?

The reward for bullying comes from three places. The victim, the bystanders, and from oversight. If a victim responds in a submissive way, the bully or harasser gets what they want. If bystanders look the other way or enable the behavior and reward it by giving the harasser continued social status, the harasser is rewarded. If the people responsible for oversight promote the harasser, despite their behavior, the harasser is rewarded.

To get a harasser to stop, we do not need to teach the harasser it is illegal. We need to teach the people who are currently inadvertently rewarding the harasser—how exactly to stop. The good news is all those other people actually want to learn how to make harassment stop. Most people would love to learn the science of how to get unwanted behavior to stop. This information is not just for the workplace. Parents are desperate to know how to get their kids to stop doing unwanted behavior too. It is much sought-after knowledge.

Creating a Solution to Harassment That Will Really Work

We now know what we want to do—make the harassers and bullies of the world stop. We know why we want to do that for moral and practical reasons. We know how to make it happen—by removing the reward. Now, we need a strategy to make that happen.

Given the current legal framework that mandates harassment training, we should be able to piggyback the needed information on to our existing harassment training programs so that everyone learns not just that it is illegal, so they should not do it, but also, if it happens to you, how exactly do you make it stop? Not just if it happens, report it. But, here are the behavioral methods required to make a bully stop bullying you. Step by step.

Is this strategy realistic? Yes. It is geared toward our real problem. It uses a science-based solution that will really work. It is also cost effective because companies are already providing this sort of training; all we are doing is tweaking the existing trainings to include the needed missing information.

Ethical philosophy compels us to solve this problem for both moral and pragmatic reasons. Science tells us how to solve it. Critical thinking helps us create a strategy that is both cost effective and implementable— piggybacking on the existing framework.

CHAPTER 2

Combining Humanist Philosophy, Science, and Education to Create More Diverse Workforces

Question

How can we use science, humanistic philosophy, and education to help companies reap the benefits of diverse workplaces while avoiding the problems caused by diversity?

Overview

What are the benefits and challenges of employing a diverse workforce? Can we use behavioral science and humanistic philosophy to help businesses reap the benefits of a diverse workforce while avoiding the problems that arise when working with a group of diverse individuals? How can we use science to eliminate problems with discrimination, harassment, and retaliation, which make the creation of truly diverse workforces so difficult to achieve?

To successfully change corporate culture to be more inclusive, we need philosophy to provide people with adequate reasons why it benefits them personally to embrace a diverse workforce. This is a challenge that is best addressed through the use of humanistic philosophy. Once a work team has decided to embrace diversity, they then need to learn specific skills and techniques to defuse the conflicts that arise and to effectively deal with harassment and discrimination so that all employees feel protected in the workgroup. These skills and techniques are best addressed by applying behavioral science techniques to the problem behaviors.

The Problem

Diverse workforces benefit employers and employees,[14] but attempts to create diverse workforces are hampered by a myriad of problems.

People coming from diverse backgrounds have different life experiences, different triggers, different world views, different assumptions, and different goals. How we talk to one another respectfully and further understand what is being said is not always easy. We all have implicit biases[15] that may prevent us from accurately perceiving the other person and their motives.

Our difficulty in seeing other people accurately and without bias is hampered by the fact that humans, as a species, are tribal animals. We instinctually feel safe around people we perceive to be like us and are frightened by those we perceive to be *other*.[16] There are a variety of ways our tribal instincts can be triggered, but once they are triggered, creating a cohesive group out of diverse individuals becomes exponentially harder.

Humanistic philosophy can help us bridge those differences. It helps us bring the *other* person into a common tribe, which helps us to override our tribal instincts, so we can view the other person as an ethical person grounded in dignity. Humanism also provides us with a common moral language we can use to create ethical consensus and resolve differences.

Diversity problems in the workplace manifest in a variety of ways and stem from a variety of causes. This is why, diversity is such a *wicked* problem to solve, meaning a problem that has so many dimensions, it does not have a single root cause. As there is no single root cause, proposed solutions to it rarely work. Even if you successful address one root cause, the others remain.

---

[14] Etsy, et al. 1995. "Workplace Diversity." Retrieved from https://www.amazon.com/Workplace-Diversity-Managers-Competitive-Advantage/dp/1558504826

[15] Greenwald, A.G., and M.R. Banaji. 1995. "Implicit Social Cognition: Attitudes, Self-Esteem, and Stereotypes." Retrieved from http://psycnet.apa.org/record/1995-17407-001

[16] Druckman, D. 1994. "Nationalism, Patriotism, and Group Loyalty: A Social Psychological Perspective." Retrieved from https://www.jstor.org/stable/222610

A combination of humanistic philosophy and applied science can help us fix these problems collectively so that we can reap the benefit of diverse workforces.

There are three major problems we need to solve simultaneously to create diverse yet cohesive work groups.

1. We need to hire more diverse workforces.
2. We need to solve the problem of social exclusion that prevents diverse work groups from creating cohesion and leads to harassment and discrimination in the workplace.
3. We need to help people more effectively deal with and resolve disagreements so that our tribal instincts do not kick in and turn what should be a rational disagreement into an irrational divisive conflict.

The Challenge of Overcoming Implicit and Explicit Bias in Personnel Decisions

We now know that our ability and willingness to hire diverse workforces is complicated by our implicit and sometimes, explicit biases.[17] We all have biases, and our biases impact our hiring decisions, firing decisions, promotion decisions, and more. We cannot fix our diversity problem without better understanding how implicit biases work so that we can take affirmative action and hire people we would not normally hire because of our biases. Otherwise, our biases will continue to control employment decisions and our businesses will suffer as a result.

Humanistic philosophy can help us work past our biases, and science can help us develop techniques so that we can work to ensure our biases don't negatively impact our personnel decisions. There have been a number of studies on blind selection processes, and they do indeed work to improve diversity in organizations.

---

[17] Ellis, C. 1994. "Diverse Approaches to Managing Diversity." Retrieved from http://onlinelibrary.wiley.com/doi/10.1002/hrm.3930330106/full

The Challenge of Eliminating Social Exclusion

Social exclusion is the process in which individuals or people are systematically blocked from (or denied full access to) various rights, opportunities, and resources that are normally available to members of an *ingroup*.

Social exclusion can happen for a variety of reasons. Sometimes, it is a result of bias, but it can also be a result of competition for resources in the workplace where individuals may dehumanize their co-workers through bullying, a technique that helps them gain access to resources and minimize the influence their target has in the workplace.

Social exclusion appears to be the main aim of bullying or harassment. Evolutionary psychologists[18] have shown that bullying is an adaptive behavior. Bullying can be thought of as a tool of group control. People who can control access to a group through social inclusion and exclusion wield a lot of power.

Humans have an instinctual need to *belong* to in-groups, and exclusion is felt as physical pain.[19] Our instinctual fear of being socially ostracized allows bullies to manipulate group dynamics and control them. The bully might not be biased against their target; they are merely using the threat of social exclusion to control a group. They do this by marking their target tribally as *other* to encourage social exclusion of the target. Anyone who is perceived as different can be marked as *other* this way. As no one wants to be excluded, our instinct is to seek inclusion in the form of currying the favor of the person perceived to have the power to include or exclude people from the group.

To create a diverse yet cohesive workgroup, social exclusion cannot be tolerated. The challenge is how to make social exclusion behavior stop. Currently, 152 countries have laws prohibiting discrimination in the

---

[18] MacDonald, K. 1996. "What do Children Want? A Conceptualisation of Evolutionary Influences on Children's Motivation in the Peer Group." Retrieved from http://journals.sagepub.com/doi/abs/10.1177/016502549601900105

[19] Novembre, G., M. Zanon, and G. Silani. 2014. "Empathy for Social Exclusion Involves the Sensory-Discriminative Component of Pain: a Within-Subject fMRI Study." *Social Cognitive and Affective Neuroscience*. Retrieved from https://academic.oup.com/scan/article/10/2/153/1652379

workplace. Several countries and state jurisdictions mandate harassment training, and yet, harassment and discrimination continue, and vulnerable people are excluded from our workplaces as a result. Laws prohibiting discrimination are not enough.

Solving this problem will require a combination of humanistic philosophy and behavioral science. Humanistic philosophy will help us resist efforts by bullies to marginalize and label people as *other*. Behavioral science will help us extinguish the unwanted exclusionary behavior.

Scientists have known for decades how to stop unwanted behavior, including exclusionary behavior, like bullying and harassment. Specifically, the science of behavioral extinction not only explains why attempts to stop this behavior results in an escalation of behavior otherwise known as retaliation, but it provides us with the tools we need to get it to stop. We need to start applying these techniques to the problem of bullying, harassment, and discrimination so that diverse individuals are no longer subjected to social exclusion in the workplace.

The Challenge of De-Escalating Conflicts to Maintain Group Cohesion

Diverse workgroups mean that there is diversity of opinion. Problem-solving is never an easy task. People with different skills sets, knowledge bases, and experience approach problem solving differently. This is both a good thing and a bad thing. The diversity of opinion can lead to better and often more creative solutions. The downside is that these differing opinions can lead to disagreements that if they remain unresolved, can cause conflict.

When we find ourselves in conflict, our tribal biases often kick in making resolution of the disagreement harder. Unfortunately, some people have learned that, if they use bullying or aggression to stigmatize the other person, it increases the chances of their viewpoints being adopted. This technique, while a successful strategy for the person employing it, negatively impacts the problem-solving process and is experienced as harassment and discrimination by the person on the receiving end of this sort of bullying behavior. It is astonishingly harmful to rational problem-solving processes.

Thomas and Kilmann describe five approaches humans take to resolving conflict.[20] Two of these approaches are considered counterproductive. The three remaining ones form the basis of most of the advice on how to resolve conflicts.

The first step in any conflict management program is to attempt to get both sides to see each other as part of the same tribe so that the tribal aggression and defenses that are preventing rational discussion from taking place are eliminated. Humanistic philosophy is essential to this effort.

Humanism can also help us develop communication strategies to help us find common ground in the problem-solving process and to resolve disagreements by using a shared set of values and moral approach. In other words, it can help us agree on why solving the problem is important and what an ideal solution should look like. This shared grounding in morality makes discussions of possible solutions more rational and less tribal.

Science should also be employed. We can use the same behavioral techniques we use to eliminate bullying and harassment to de-escalate conflict behavior to set the stage for humanistic communication strategies to take root. We can also use what is learned from sociology on group dynamics and decision-making to help us better manage disagreements so that they do not devolve into conflict. The goal is to help teams focus on collaborative problem-solving as a team, instead of allowing the team to fracture into warring tribes.

Transformative Approach

Philosophy on its own is not enough, and science on its own is not enough. Combining philosophy, science, and education can create positive social change in corporate culture.

Humanistic philosophy helps us tweak our thinking so that we can overcome our biases, see our colleagues as members of our in-group/tribe, and encourages us to be compassionate and patient with them

---

[20] Thomas, K.W., and R.H. Kilmann. 2015. "An Overview of the Thomas-Kilmann Conflict Mode Instrument (TKI)." Retrieved from http://kilmanndiagnostics.com/overview-thomas-kilmann-conflict-mode-instrument-tki

when disagreements arise. It also provides us with the motivation and the knowledge we need to resist attempts by bullies to manipulate us through social exclusion.

Science can provide us with a complimentary toolset needed to resist our biases, so they no longer control our decision-making processes. We can use behavioral science strategies to establish new cultural norms that reinforce respectful behavior in the workplace and collaborative problem-solving. We can also use behavioral science to help eliminate social exclusionary behavior that prevents diverse work groups from becoming cohesive.

A holistic approach that combines the best of humanistic philosophy with applied science can help us transform our approach so that the promise of social inclusion becomes a reality.

Creating a Strategy

If we were to create a strategy to create this sort of cultural change within an organization, it would be multipronged. It would need to help us recruit more diverse individuals. It would require us to build into our systems protection for those new individuals to help them stay and flourish and not allow tribal divisions to drive them out. And, we would have to nurture a culture of collaborative ethical problem-solving that focuses, not on tribal alliances, but on effective ethical problem-solving.

An implementable strategy would incorporate new hiring policies and systems. Training for all staff on the necessary skills and philosophic inclusionary thinking and benefits. Specific training for executive leadership and HR on how to help coach people through the transition. Training for mid-level management on expectations on how to manage and encourage diverse work groups. I would probably also implement culture ambassador groups that include people from all levels of the organization and have them meet regularly to discuss implementation problems and ways to fix them. This would help provide ongoing monitoring to ensure that bullying and social exclusion are not happening, and if they are, it is shut down and the problem person eliminated from the workplace, as well as help to ensure that problems at the bottom of the organization are surfaced and dealt with at the highest levels of the organization (in other words make it so that the staff have the ability to communicate directly with executive leadership if they need to bypass a problem manager.

For this to happen, it would require a commitment from executive leadership to see this process through to the end. Without that commitment, this sort of attempted organizational cultural change would probably fail.

For problems with multiple dimensions, a realistic strategy will require multiple sub-strategies integrated into a holistic strategy. It would also include a commitment to incorporating shared ethical values into all aspects of decision-making and problem-solving.

To solve the problem of diverse work groups, we need ethical philosophy to help us get past our biases and tribal alliances. We need science to help us understand why we are having problems and what solutions will work, and we need to provide ongoing education in the form of training and ongoing coaching to ensure that the cultural shifts and behavioral changes required have time to take root and grow. And we again, need ethical philosophy to help ground all discussions, decision-making, and problem-solving using the outcomes of well-being and flourishing as a guide.

About the Author

Jennifer Hancock is a mom, author of several books, and founder of Humanist Learning Systems. Jennifer is unique in that she was raised as a freethinker and is considered one of the top speakers and writers in the world of Humanism today. Her professional background is varied including stints in both the for-profit and non-profit sectors. She has served as Director of Volunteer Services for the Los Angeles SPCA, sold international franchise licenses for a biotech firm, was the Manager of Acquisition Group Information for a ½ billion dollar company and served as the executive director for the Humanists of Florida. When she became a mother, she decided to stay at home. But that didn't last long. Shortly after her son was born, she published her first book, The Humanist Approach to Happiness: Practical Wisdom. Her speaking and teaching business coalesced into the founding of Humanist Learning Systems which provides online personal and professional development training in humanistic business management and science-based harassment training that actually works.

Index

OTHER TITLES IN OUR BUSINESS ETHICS AND CORPORATE CITIZENSHIP COLLECTION

David Wasieleski, Editor

- *Engaging Millennials for Ethical Leadership: What Works For Young Professionals and Their Managers* by Jessica McManus Warnell
- *Sales Ethics: How To Sell Effectively While Doing the Right Thing* by Alberto Aleo and Alice Alessandri
- *Working Ethically in Finance: Clarifying Our Vocation* by Anthony Asher
- *A Strategic and Tactical Approach to Global Business Ethics, Second Edition* by Lawrence A. Beer
- *Shaping the Future of Work: What Future Worker, Business, Government, and Education Leaders Need To Do For All To Prosper* by Thomas A. Kochan
- *War Stories: Fighting, Competing, Imagining, Leading* by Leigh Hafrey
- *Social Media Ethics Made Easy: How to Comply with FTC Guidelines* by Joseph W. Barnes
- *Adapting to Change: The Business of Climate Resilience* by Ann Goodman
- *Educating Business Professionals: The Call Beyond Competence and Expertise* by Lana S. Nino and Susan D. Gotsch
- *Powerful Performance: How to Be Influential, Ethical, and Successful in Business* by Mark Eyre

Announcing the Business Expert Press Digital Library

Concise e-books business students need for classroom and research

This book can also be purchased in an e-book collection by your library as

- a one-time purchase,
- that is owned forever,
- allows for simultaneous readers,
- has no restrictions on printing, and
- can be downloaded as PDFs from within the library community.

Our digital library collections are a great solution to beat the rising cost of textbooks. E-books can be loaded into their course management systems or onto students' e-book readers.
The **Business Expert Press** digital libraries are very affordable, with no obligation to buy in future years. For more information, please visit **www.businessexpertpress.com/librarians**. To set up a trial in the United States, please email **sales@businessexpertpress.com**.